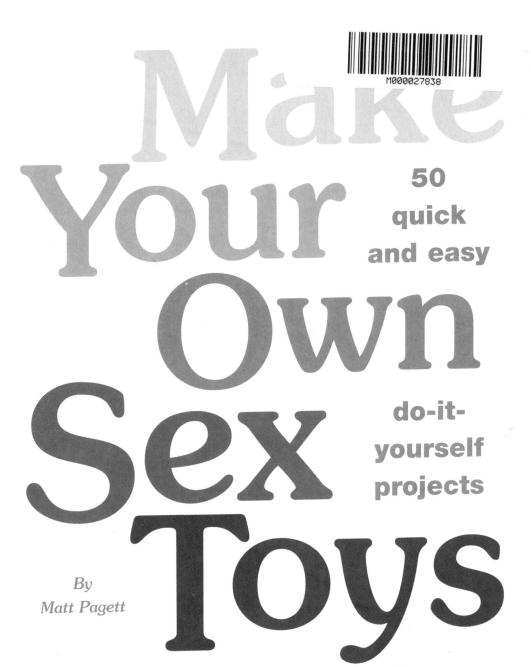

Make Your Own Sex Toys

50 quick and easy do-it-yourself projects

By
Matt Pagett

CHRONICLE BOOKS
SAN FRANCISCO

First published in the United States in 2007 by Chronicle Books LLC.
First published in the United Kingdom in 2007 by Crombie Jardine.

Library of Congress Cataloging-in-Publication Data available.

ISBN-10: 0-8118-5581-3
ISBN-13: 978-0-8118-5581-5

Manufactured in Singapore

Conceived and produced by Quid Publishing
Level 4, Sheridan House
114 Western Road
Hove BN3 1DD
www.quidpublishing.com
Designed by Lindsey Johns

Distributed in Canada by Raincoast Books
9050 Shaughnessy Street
Vancouver, British Columbia V6P 6E5

10 9 8 7 6 5 4 3 2 1

Chronicle Books LLC
680 Second Street
San Francisco, California 94107

www.chroniclebooks.com

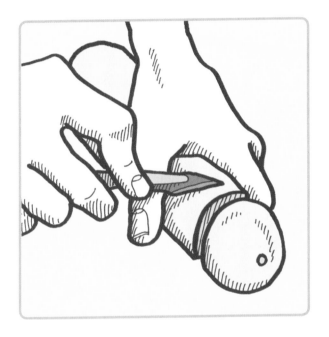

"I'd like to thank Amy, James, Nigel, Lindsey, Sam, and Jen, and all who suggested new toys and ways of using them. This book is dedicated to lovers and players everywhere."

Contents

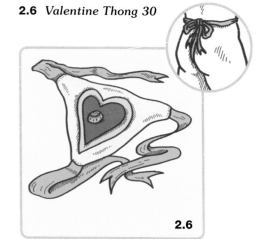

2.6

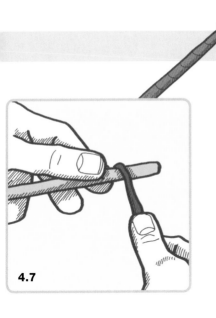

4.7

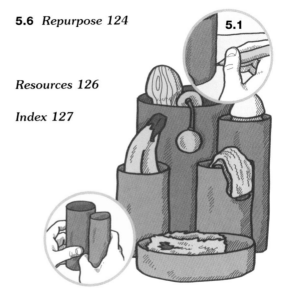

5.1

5 **Storage and Organizers** 113

4 **For Couples** 83

Introduction

A Warm Welcome

Sex. It's everywhere. From the highest mountain to the deepest ocean, where there is life, there is sex. If we're not doing it, we're thinking about it. If we're not thinking about it, we're dreaming about it. If we're not dreaming about it, we're Mother Teresa— i.e., celibate and/or dead.

Sex is the great thrusting engine that drives mankind forward, and just as every engine needs fuel and maintenance, so your sex life deserves some love and attention. Sex toys have a long history (see pages 10–11) and have played their part in the lubrication of that engine for thousands of years, right up to the present day. Indeed, new devices for the twenty-first century are evolving apace, taking advantage of technological advances that lead to mind-boggling possibilities, such as intercontinental penetration, teledildonics, and digital orgasms, to name a few.

Keen and Green
Even a trip to the local grocery store can bear fruit (and vegetables!) for the DIY sex-toy enthusiast.

★ ★ ★

"Say good-bye to furtive trips to sleazy shops or hours of wading through gross Internet pages—everything you need is here!"

★ ★ ★

This book, however, aims to offer you a quiet space to experiment and explore in a more intimate, innocent, and inexpensive way, whether you're going solo or with a partner. Away from the brash, aggressive marketing of the modern sex industry, *Make Your Own Sex Toys* gives you tips, suggestions, and advice on how to heighten your pleasure with fun, creativity, and style.

The book's three main sections are For Him, For Her, and For Couples. Each double-page spread features a toy that can easily be made using objects readily available, if not around the house, then certainly from your local stores. Say good-bye to furtive trips to sleazy shops or hours of wading though gross Internet pages—everything you need is here! With useful illustrations guiding you through your crafting, every toy also has its own time estimation, a difficulty rating, and a list of what materials you'll need. Tips, handy hints, and budget options also help you on your way. The book finishes with a storage section, advising you on the best way to keep your toys as fresh and clean as the day they were made.

Whether you're a dedicated professional or an amateur enthusiast, there is something here for everyone. Welcome to the world of sex toys, DIY style.

Happy Together
And it's not just for loners. Making your own can help put the magic back into even the most jaded relationships.

The Basics

The world of making your own sex

toys is both fascinating and varied,

but there are some important facts

you'll need to know before you get

your hands sticky.

1.1

Sex Toy History

It is said that every generation likes to think they were the first ones to have sex. Well, while previous civilizations and generations may not have had the Rabbit Habit to buzz themselves to oblivion, rest assured they tried their best.

23,000 BC
The so-called Venus of Willendorf is one of the earliest examples of prehistoric sculpture. With emphasis on the breasts, buttocks, and vaginal lips, this faceless stone icon could be a fertility goddess, or an early porn star.

500 BC
Documents found in the Greek port of Miletus mention the use of "olisbos," an early form of dildo. Greek vase decorations also feature double-ended dildos.

AD 300
The *Kama Sutra* mentions penis extensions; made from materials such as gold, leather, and buffalo horn, they were designed to make men look that little bit bigger.

1200s
The first proto-cockring originates from China. The eyelids of a goat were used at the base, and the lashes, still intact, were kept hard and useful for the lady's heightened pleasure during intercourse. The identity of the person who saw a goat's eye and thought, "Wouldn't mind having that 'round my cock," remains a mystery. Four hundred years later, rings were made from ivory, which was ornately carved with dragons whose tongues sometimes extended for female arousal.

Goat to Extremes
Chinese goats will have welcomed the arrival of ivory cockrings.

1750
In Europe, brothels specializing in flagellation from a dominatrix laid the roots for modern S&M practice. In 1791, the Marquis de Sade published *Justine*, a novel featuring heavy debauchery involving whips, nipple clamps, restraints, and so on.

1869
American George Taylor invented the first steam-powered vibrator. Cumbersome to say the least, it was used to ease the symptoms of female

patients with "hysteria" (what is now called "sexual arousal"). The machine massaged the woman in question, making lives easier for the physicians treating them, who previously had to do it by hand. Thirteen years later, Joseph Mortimer Granville developed an electromechanical vibrator for massaging the injuries of male patients in the U.K.

Blow Buddy?
While looking distinctly like a hair dryer, this is in fact one of the earliest vibrators. Hardly discreet...

Late 1800s/Early 1900s
Film and theater became more sexualized, with early porn and striptease shows. Various props like dildos, vibrators, fans, and erotic clothing were incorporated into, and popularized by, the acts.

Early 1900s
Plug-in vibrators were developed as some of the first electrified home appliances, though they were still marketed for women to ease "hysteria," as well as for other health and relaxation uses.

1930s
Campaigns by various moral guardians, incensed by the increase in women seeking mechanical means to bliss, forced the closure of many vibrator manufacturers. Vibrators all but disappeared for some years.

In the same period, the development of latex rubber helped to revolutionize contraception, sex-toy manufacture, and thus the whole approach to sex.

Early 1960s
Vibrators began to reemerge after the American Medical Association declared that hysteria was not, after all, an ailment and women could be seen as sexual beings with their own desires and needs.

Late 1900s/Early 2000s
The development of camera and video technology meant more could be done at home, eliminating the need for third-party involvement. Porn led the way.

1998
Alabama outlawed the sale of sex toys, and a few other states soon followed suit. A completely understandable, right-thinking law: why buy them when you can make your own?

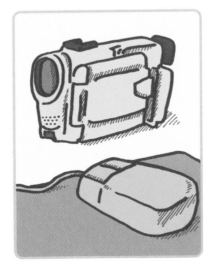

2007
The Internet has opened eyes much wider, making new experiences just a click away: orgasms at certain pre-programmed times of the day, sex with someone in a totally different country, and all the porn you can shake a throbbing stick at.

Turn Me On
Anyone can be a secret porn star. Just press the right buttons, then point and play.

Measuring Up: Him

Gentlemen! This book is all about heightening sexual pleasure, so familiarize yourself with your raw materials to get the most from your DIY sex-toy creations.

Mind
While all may be working fine down below, the real professional should also use his brain to keep control of any unbridled lust resulting from sex-toy overload.

Heart
Check, too, that you're feeling up to the job. Emotional baggage can fog the freshest experience.

Butt
The gluteus maximus can be displayed to maximum effect by donning a Valentine Thong (see page 30).

Waist
Taking a careful waist measurement (between the rib cage and the hips) is essential for toys such as the Crochet Restrictor (see page 42). The waist size from your favorite pair of jeans will not be sufficiently accurate.

Penis
Diligent measuring of length and girth (see opposite) will lead to enhanced enjoyment and satisfaction. An extra inch here will benefit only your ego.

Scrotum
All cockrings should fit around the base of the penis and scrotum, as measured nearest the body. Anywhere else, and they just don't look or feel as good.

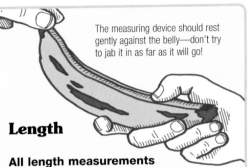

The measuring device should rest gently against the belly—don't try to jab it in as far as it will go!

Length

All length measurements indicated in this book are based on the length of one's manhood at full tumescence.

1 Excite yourself to your full capacity.

2 Place a tape measure or ruler at the root of your manhood, on the topside, where it meets your body.

3 Note the distance at the tip. Write this down.

4 For accuracy, take three readings over three days, add them together, and divide by three. (Erection sizes can vary depending on numerous factors, such as time of day, previous sexual activity, and so on.)

Girth

Similarly, all girth measurements refer to you at your hardest state.

1 Excite yourself to full capacity.

2 Place a piece of string around the thickest part of your erection. Wrap it around your circumference once.

3 Mark off the point where the ends of the string meet, and measure that length with a ruler.

4 Again, repeat this exercise on three consecutive days and take an average for an exact reading.

Wind the string ONCE ONLY around your penis, and don't pull it too tight.

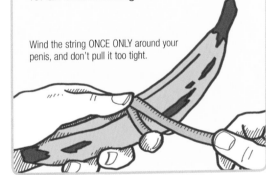

★ ★

It's What You Do With It That Counts

Penile dimensions have long been a source of debate and inquiry. Since the first medical investigation into the matter was conducted in 1942, questions have been raised about how the measurement should be taken (e.g., should the subject be flaccid or erect or stretched), from where the measurement should be taken (the underside or the topside, as near to the pubic bone as possible or lightly resting against the belly), how many subjects need to be measured to ensure accuracy, and who does the measuring anyway. Safe to say, if you've got a penis less than 11", get yourself to your doctor (kidding).

1.3

Measuring Up: Her

Ladies! Knowing what you're working with can make a world of difference, so follow this easy-to-use guide and you can't go wrong.

Head
The brain is the largest sexual organ, and controls the release of chemicals that make orgasms possible. Mental engagement is as important as anything else, if not more so.

Heart
Head say go, heart say no? Trust your instinct and fulfillment will be all the greater.

Hips
Toys such as the Strap-On Salami (see page 108) depend on accurate measurements being taken, so best get it right from the start.

Breasts
Big, small, hulking, or delicate—they come in all shapes and sizes. However they look, you could do a lot worse than give them a golden covering (see page 72).

Nipples
Stimulation or sexual arousal can make your teats complete. Start gently and you may not need the tape to stick on your nipple tassels (see page 58) after all.

Vagina
What goes up won't necessarily come back down with similar ease. Avoid unnecessary embarrassment and discomfort by ensuring all inserted objects can be removed safely.

The Clitoris

The clitoris is the only organ in the human body (either male or female) whose sole purpose is to transmit sexual sensation.

Who are we to stand in its way? The head (that sensitive little button where the tops of the labia meet) has roughly four times as many sensory nerve endings as the head of the penis. Now, if only you had a toy for it to play with . . .

There are various piercings available for the more adventurous, the most common being the vertical or horizontal hood piercings. As the names suggest, only the surrounding hood is spiked, rather than the clitoris itself, and reports on the degree to which they increase arousal are mixed. Any such adornment should be performed by a registered professional—i.e., you won't find any ice-cube/safety-pin explanations in this book.

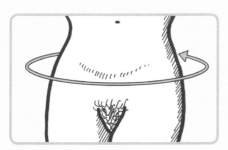

Waist Not Want Not
Honest and accurate waist measurement is required—don't deny that extra inch.

The G-Spot

The sexual Holy Grail, the G-spot, is a source of great mystery and pleasure. Both men and women try to find it, with varying degrees of success.

The elusive G-spot, named after German gynecologist Ernst Gräfenburg, is the spongy tissue surrounding a woman's urethra that can be felt through the top wall of the vagina, about two inches inside. Direct G-spot stimulation often causes greater enjoyment than clitoral frottage, promoting a more vigorous and intense orgasm.

Its sourcing is easier when the owner is aroused, and it can be stroked or stimulated phallically. A sizeable amount of foreplay is advisable before any attempt to find it is made, and while some research will bear fruit in minutes, you may need to persevere for an hour or more. The accompanying orgasm, if reached, will lead to possible secretion, even ejaculation. Since that quest often requires steady, extended pressure that a penis or even a hand can't manage for too long, many penetrative sex toys are specifically designed to target the G-Spot. However, it's worth noting that some women feel nothing at all when this area is poked, while others find it annoying or painful. The most important element to consider in seeking the hidden treasure is to have fun—and a few DIY toys may just help in the hunt.

1.4

Health & Safety

It must be remembered that, as well as being the source of great joy and satisfaction, the genital area, both male and female, is a potential harbinger of physical doom and gloom. Attention should be paid to good hygiene at all times. Follow these guidelines and your toying around will continue unblemished.

Sexual Health

Adhere to the following guidelines when using any sex toy. If in doubt, use common sense and proceed with caution—that way you can enjoy the rich rewards this book offers with creativity and fun!

● After use, always wash the toys with soap and warm water. Store in a clean, dry place.

● Any penetrative toy should be covered with at least one condom.

● If the same toy is to be used by a different partner, or go from one orifice to another, use a new condom.

● The tissue of the anal passage is delicate and prone to tearing; use plenty of lubrication for any anal insertions.

● Objects designed for anal insertion must always have a base larger than the shaft, to prevent object disappearance. Such disappearances can prove uncomfortable, embarrassing, and dangerous.

● Remove all tampons before sexual activity begins.

Keep It Clean
Not only useful for good hygiene, male readers may be interested to learn some new tricks with an old bar of soap (page 20).

Feminine Hygiene
Prince Charles once expressed the desire to be Camilla's tampon, but it's a better idea to avoid tampons altogether.

DIY Health

These general guidelines should be adhered to when following the projects contained in this book. Where more specific safety precautions are advisable, these have been included along with the project itself.

● Be sensible when using sharp objects or cutting implements.

● Ensure all work surfaces are clean and free from clutter before embarking on any project.

● Wash your hands both before and after making a toy.

Just A Small Prick?
Warning! Hidden sharp objects can take you straight to the ER.

● Always use nontoxic paints, glues, and other materials. In all cases, defer to the manufacturer's instructions and warnings.

● Anything designed for insertion should always be covered with at least one coat of nontoxic lacquer, varnish, or similar and allowed to dry thoroughly before use. Always cover these objects with a condom.

● Keep all toys in a clean environment once they have been used and washed (see pages 113—125 for storage ideas).

● Ensure any stitched or knitted objects are clear of any pins, needles, and so on before use.

● Always use common sense. If something gives you a rash, feels uncomfortable, seems unsafe, or otherwise doesn't make you a happy camper, just don't do it.

Choosing Lubricants

Lubricants come in various forms, but only silicone- or water-based ones (such as Astroglide or K-Y) can be safely used with condoms. Oil-based lube can rot and/or weaken the rubber that condoms are made from, and should be avoided.

For Him

From holes in the most innocent

of spaces to underwear that fits

in all the right places, everything

the resourceful male sex-toy fan

should need is here.

2.1

Soapy Suds

Get yourself in a lather with this utterly simple toy. Easy to make, easy to use, and great for personal hygiene. Sex doesn't have to be dirty with Soapy Suds! This bubbly number is a simple yet effective aid to bring you to completion during your ablutions.

Time to Create:
10 minutes

Skill Level:
Intermediate

You Will Need:
1 large bar of regular soap (the larger the better), felt-tip pen or marker, household drill, no. 8 drill bit, vise, craft knife

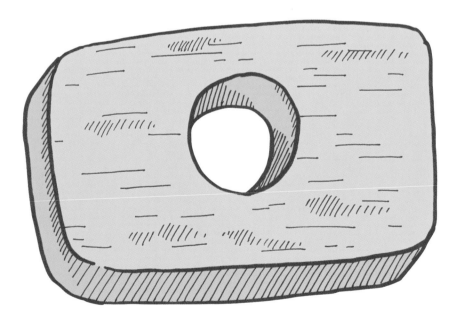

Foam Alone
All you need is a hole of the right size and a splash of water for lubrication, and you can have a thoroughly clean time.

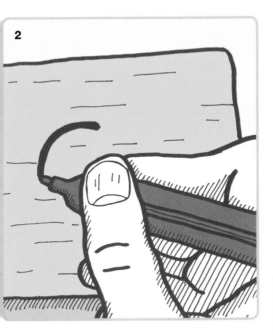

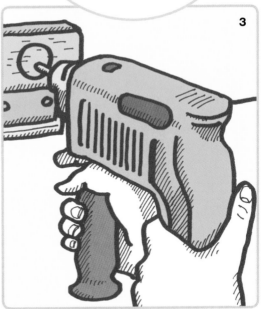

★ ★ ★

Fancy That

Once the hole has gotten too big, take advantage of the fact that the soap still retains its cleansing properties!

★ ★ ★

Method:

1 Ensure the bar of soap is dry. Any wetness could cause the drill to slip and lead to an accident.

2 As discussed in Measuring Up (see page 13), measure your girth, then draw a corresponding circle onto the middle of the soap with a felt-tip pen or marker.

3 Having secured it in a vise or similar, use a drill to gently bore a hole all the way through the soap. Once the hole has been made, you can then use a craft knife to make it larger. It's better to make it too small than too big at this stage.

4 Once completed, the toy is ready for use in the shower or bath. Work up a good lather with plenty of water and plenty of friction. The hole's edges and each tiny bubble will stimulate and massage you to a luxurious climax.

Fruity-Scoopy

A warm, fleshy, sensual experience awaits users of the Fruity-Scoopy. Think American Pie *meets fruit salad. For those with roommates, maybe best not to keep it in the fridge afterward.*

Time to Create:
15 minutes

Skill Level:
Intermediate

You Will Need:
1 ripe melon (e.g., cantaloupe, honeydew), felt-tip pen or marker, melon baller (or sharp-edged spoon), microwave, lubricant

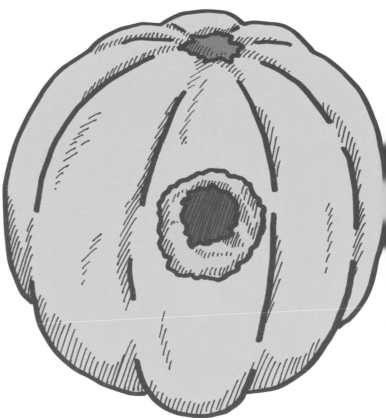

Scoop and Shoot
The humble melon, so beloved of fruit cognoscenti, provides amazing, lifelike results upon entry into the world of the DIY sex-toy enthusiast.

3

4

Method:

1 Buy a good-sized melon, the riper the better. A good way of determining ripeness is to smell the fruit in-store before you buy—if you can detect the aroma, it's ready.

2 Once you're back home (and not before), mark a circle corresponding to your measured girth (see page 13) directly onto the melon with a felt-tip pen or marker.

3 With the melon baller, carefully dig a hole to the fruit's center, removing any seeds you find along the way (unless you want to explain to the ER nurse why you've got a melon seed lodged in your urethra). You might also want to peel away any skin lingering around the hole's opening—it's not as friction-friendly as the melon's fleshy interior.

4 Microwave the melon to raise it to body temperature, but no hotter or you may get scalded. Depending on the microwave and the size of the melon, about 30 seconds should be enough.

★ ★ ★ ★ ★ ★ ★ ★ ★ ★ ★

A Quicker Alternative

Using a watermelon this time, simply split it in two, carve out the right amount of flesh, and run the fruit under some hot water before penetration. This provides a similar sensation for gentlemen on the go.

★ ★ ★ ★ ★ ★ ★ ★ ★ ★ ★

5 Squirt some lube into the hole and you're ready! The warm, soft flesh of the melon yields to your tumescence, heightening the pleasure sensation. As close to the real thing as you could possibly get.

2.3

A Bubble-Wrap Blow

Everyone loves to pop the bubbles on sheets of Bubble Wrap. Well, here's even more fun for the man who's less than satisfied with his package (and would rather play with the wrapping).

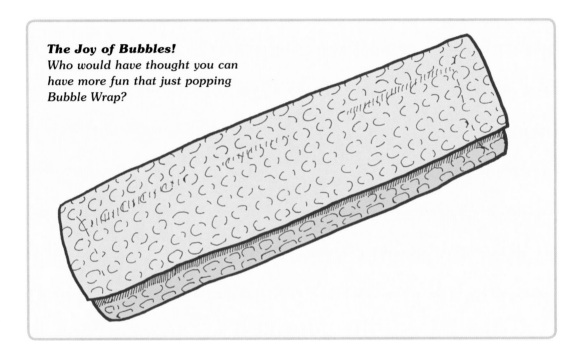

The Joy of Bubbles!
Who would have thought you can have more fun that just popping Bubble Wrap?

 Time to Create:
3 minutes (assuming that all materials are easily located)

Skill Level:
Intermediate

 You Will Need:
Bubble Wrap (a sheet measuring 12" x 12" should be fine), towel (a flannel or folded t-shirt will also work), baby oil or personal lubricant

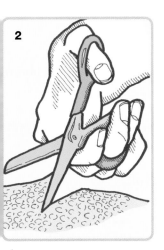

Method:

1 Make sure that the Bubble Wrap you are using is clean and free from any staples or other objects that could cause obstructions.

2 Using the Measuring Up guide (see page 13), take a pair of scissors and cut the Bubble Wrap into the same dimensions as your extended girth.

3 Roll the made-to-measure Bubble Wrap into a cylinder shape with the bubbles on the inside surface.

4 Take the towel (or any other suitable—and washable—fabric item that you can find) and wrap this around the cylindrical Bubble-Wrap tube.

5 When you are physically ready to use your bubble toy, smear the inside of the cylinder with personal lubricant.

6 Sit back, relax, and enjoy the stimulation of hundreds of bubbles: each one massaging and caressing to deliver a highly sensuous and fulfilling result.

★ ★ ★ ★ ★ ★ ★ ★ ★ ★ ★ ★ ★ ★

Handy Hint

Don't just chuck your used sex toys in the trash. As the saying goes: Reduce, Reuse, Recycle. For the environmentally aware, the Bubble-Wrap Blow can be washed out and reused as and when you feel like it. Alternatively, if you prefer, why not wind down by popping some of the bubbles?

★ ★ ★ ★ ★ ★ ★ ★ ★ ★ ★ ★ ★ ★

2.4

Sloppy Sock

One of life's eternal questions: what to do with all those odd socks? A possible answer is provided here—get sloppy!

Time to Create:
2 minutes

Skill Level:
Beginner

You Will Need:
1 sock, 1 surgical glove or condom, lubricant

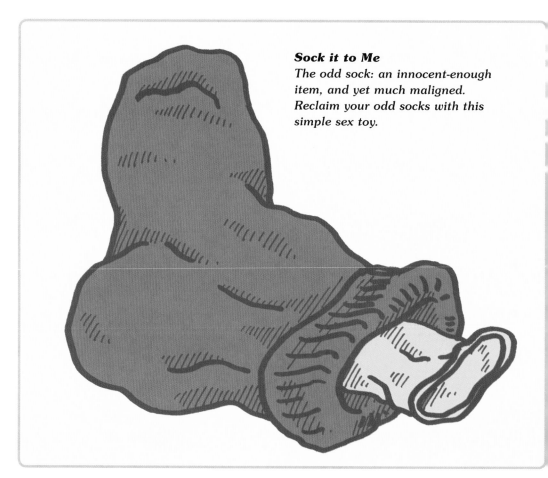

Sock it to Me
The odd sock: an innocent-enough item, and yet much maligned. Reclaim your odd socks with this simple sex toy.

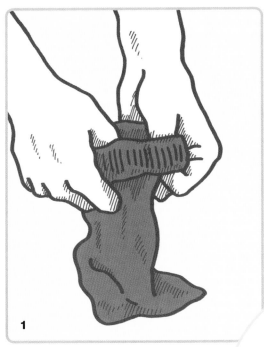

1

Method:

1 Take a sock and roll the top down to just above the ankle.

2 Place the glove or condom inside, then squeeze in a decent amount of lube.

3 The sock provides a good grip as you rise to the occasion. You may also want to place it between two objects, like cushions, leaving your hands free to play with your nipples, for example.

★ ★ ★

Top Tip

Any spillages and seepages can be mopped up using the sock afterward.

★ ★ ★

2

As Simple as They Come
Just two easy steps and you're ready. For the sock or foot fetishist, extra pleasure may be derived from knowing whose sock it is, its color, smell, and so on.

2.5

Knitted Willy Warmer

If you're an expert at knitting, this charming Willy Warmer is a fun project you can make quickly and easily. If you've never knitted before, this is an easy item that will teach all the basics. So get knitting and banish those winter blues!

 **Time to Create:** 60 minutes (depending on your knitting ability)

 Skill Level: Beginner— Intermediate

 You Will Need 2-ounce ball of double-knit wool, size 3 tapestry needle

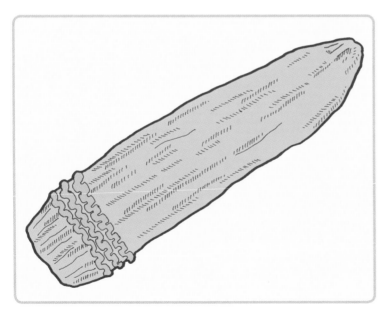

Illustrations 1–4 (right) show you how to knit your first row:

1 Insert your right needle into the first stitch.

2 Bring yarn over the right needle's point using your right index finger.

3 Fetch the yarn through the stitch.

4 Slip the loop on the left needle over to the right needle, and that's one stitch made. Carry on until the whole of the first row is now on the right needle, and then turn it around and start as before.

Warm and Cozy
A fine toy that is surely something of a design classic. The advanced knitter may want to create a multicolored warmer, but remember: fleshy colors can alarm unsuspecting partners.

1

2

3

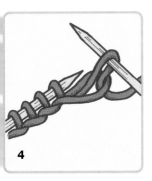

4

Method:

For the Cuff:

1 Using size 3 double-pointed needles and long-tail, cast on 24 stitches.

2 Place a marker stitch, and join without twisting.

3 Round (or Row) 1: knit 1, purl 1; repeat.

4 Repeat Round (Row) 1 four times to create four rows.

For the Main Shaft:

1 Form Round 5 of the Cuff Knit.

2 Repeat Row 6 until piece measures desired length (32 rows = 6$\frac{1}{2}$").

For the Cone-End:

1 Decrease Round 1: knit 2, knit together, knit 2; repeat from 20 stitches.

2 Even Rounds: Knit.

3 Decrease Round 3: knit 1, knit together, knit 2; repeat from 16 stitches.

4 Decrease Round 5: knit together, knit 1; repeat from 12 stitches.

5 Decrease Round 7: knit together 6 times. 6 stitches.

6 Cut yarn.

7 Use tapestry needle to run tail through remaining stitches and pull closed.

⋆ ⋆ ⋆

Top Tip

This may seem daunting for the beginner. Why not research more on the Internet or in your local library? It will be worth the effort and, come winter, your willy will be thanking you.

⋆ ⋆ ⋆

2.6

Valentine Thong

Boxers or briefs? Neither will impress the object of your affection quite as much as this beautifully crafted posing pouch.

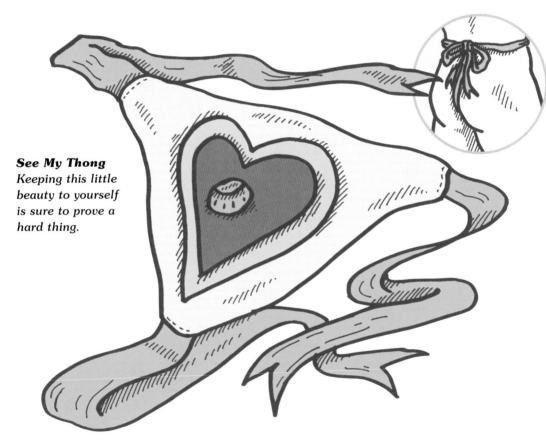

See My Thong
Keeping this little beauty to yourself is sure to prove a hard thing.

Time to Create:
35 minutes

Skill Level:
Advanced

You Will Need:
1 piece cotton cloth (at least 10" x 10"), 2 pieces differently colored felt (at least 5" x 5" each), scissors, glue, 1 jewel, 3 ribbons, needle and thread

2

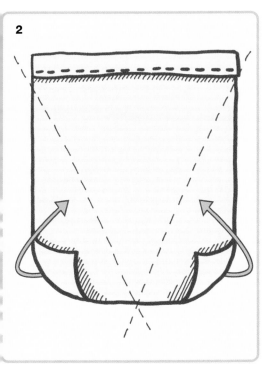

Method:

1 Cut a square piece of cotton cloth (size will vary according to package size and desired skimpiness). Fold just under half an inch over the top edge and stitch in place.

2 From nearly halfway along the bottom edge back to the top two corners, fold the two sides and stitch the fabric where it meets. You should be left with a basic pouch shape.

3 Cut out two hearts from the felt, one (A) slightly larger then the other (B). Glue B onto A, add the jewel to the center of B, and then glue the whole decoration onto the cotton pouch.

4 Once the glue is dry, you then need to sew the ribbons onto the three pouch corners. The ribbons need to tie comfortably around the waist and up through the butt crack, so ensure they are long enough.

5 When all is secure, the pouch is ready to wear.

3–4

A   **B**

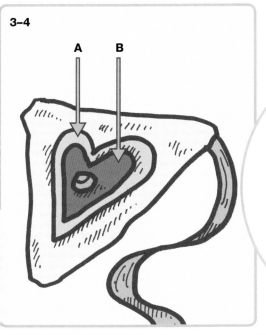

★ ★ ★

Of course, the decorations illustrated here are only suggestions. Why not choose your own, or experiment with different options—e.g., metal studs, spikes, plastic flowers, or sequins? Let your imagination run wild!

★ ★ ★

2.7

Resistance Is Futile

Ronald Reagan once urged us to "resolve that we will stop spreading dependency and start spreading opportunity; that we will stop spreading bondage and start spreading freedom." The man had obviously never used these delightful bondage straps.

Deceptive Appearances
They may look pretty, but once in use, these cuffs are certain to unleash your harsher side.

Time to Create:
10 minutes

Skill Level:
Beginner

You Will Need:
2 strips of fabric (at least 2" x 10"), scissors, 2 Velcro strips, needle and thread, 2 brass rings or similar

Method:

1 Measure the circumference of your wrist.

2 Add an extra inch and cut an appropriate length of fabric. Hem each end to prevent fraying in the future.

3 Attach one part of the Velcro pair to one end of the cuff and the other part of the pair to the other end of the cuff. Although some Velcro has an adhesive backing, it is better to sew it on as this allows for a greater amount of struggle, resistance, and so on.

4 In the middle of the strap, sew on one of the brass rings.

5 Repeat steps 2 through 4 to make the second strap, and you now have a beautiful pair of handcrafted restraint cuffs.

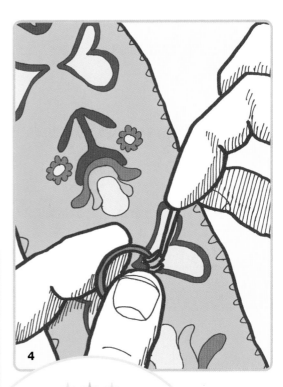

4

3

★ ★ ★

Top Tip

Why stop at the wrists? The same method can be used for ankle cuffs, and even, for the more adventurous, a full body harness.

★ ★ ★

2.8

Bolo Ring

Since ancient times, man has used rings and straps to enhance his pleasure. Pressure, when applied to the blood vessels at the base, engorges the penis, heightening sensation. This rubber ring could well be a simpler alternative to the little blue pill.

Time to Create:
10 minutes

Skill Level:
Intermediate

You Will Need:
1 strip of elastic (at least 1" wide), scissors, 1 snap, needle and thread or a snap-attaching tool

Tight Fit
The Bolo Ring's strong elastic works against the increased blood flow. If it all gets too much, just be sure to snap it off before you pass out . . .

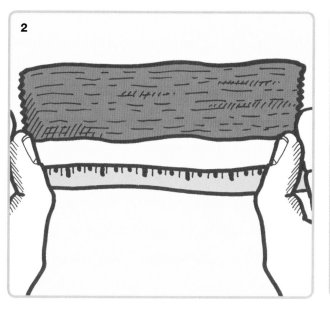

Method:

1 Measure your girth according to the guide on page 13.

2 Add an extra inch and cut a corresponding piece of elastic.

3 Attach the snap at the required position. It can usually be sewn on, but a far easier and quicker method is to use a snap-attaching tool, widely available and inexpensive at craft stores.

Bingo!

You now possess a secure and effective way to make you feel even more of a man than you do already.

★ ★

Cheaper Thrills

Suffer from fumbling fingers? Just use a rubber band or two.
And remember that such toys, however they're made,
should always sit at the very base of the penis and scrotum.

★ ★

2.9

Teste Tickler

The addition of some fake fur ensures this cockring answers the call of the wild and heightens your inner animal. Go feral and keep growling.

Roooaaaarrr!
The lion will be doing anything BUT sleeping when you slip this furry number around the base of your own best friend.

Time to Create:
10 minutes

Skill Level:
Intermediate

You Will Need:
2 pieces of fake fur (at least 2" x 8"), scissors, glue, 1 snap, needle and thread or a snap-attaching tool

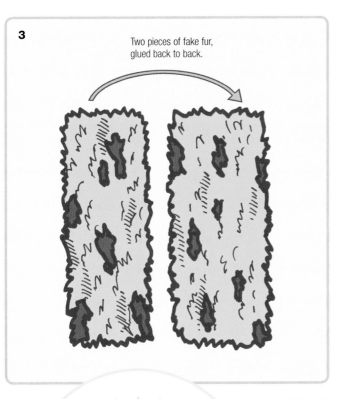

3

Two pieces of fake fur, glued back to back.

Method:

1 Measure your girth according to the guide on page 13.

2 Add an extra inch and cut a corresponding piece of fake fur.

3 Cut a second piece of fur with the exact same dimensions. Glue the two pieces together back to back.

4 Once the glue is dry, attach one half of the snap to each end using either a needle and thread or the far easier snap-attaching tool.

5 Go get 'em, tiger! Keep the Tickler clean and fresh with regular fluffing and brushing.

★ ★ ★

Top Tip

When your Tickler needs a wash, do it by hand in cold water and gentle soap.

★ ★ ★

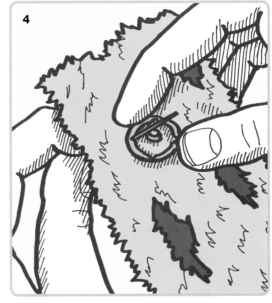

4

2.10

Silver Sleeve

A variation on the Knitted Willy Warmer (page 28), this item will keep you snug, sexy, sparkly, and looking like a million bucks.

Time to Create:
45 minutes

Skill Level:
Advanced

You Will Need:
1 piece shiny lamé fabric (at least 10" x 15"), needle and thread, ribbon, 1 safety pin

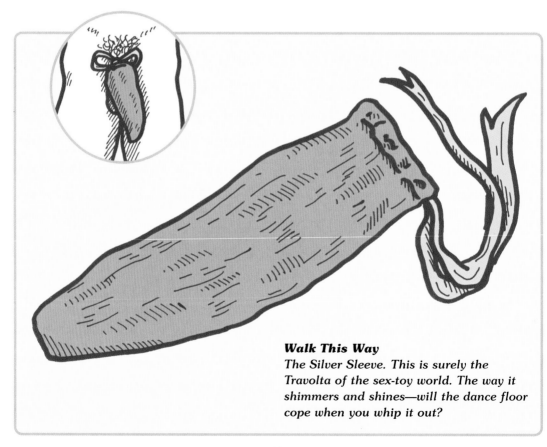

Walk This Way
The Silver Sleeve. This is surely the Travolta of the sex-toy world. The way it shimmers and shines—will the dance floor cope when you whip it out?

Method:

1 Measure your length and girth according to the guides on page 13. Then, adding 2" to both dimensions, measure and cut a corresponding piece of lamé.

2 Lay the fabric out with the longest edge leading away from you. Fold the topmost corners in toward the center, but not so they meet. Sew these two triangles into place.

3 Fold 1" over the bottom (to allow the ribbon drawstring through) and also sew into place.

4 Fold the fabric in half with the neat side inward. Sew along the top and sides, but do not sew over the drawstring's passage.

5 Turn the sleeve inside out. Fasten the safety pin to the ribbon and pass it through the top edge.

6 Pull the drawstring tight so it doesn't fall off, and remove the pin. With this silky, slithery slip-on, you will indeed be the sultan of the sheets!

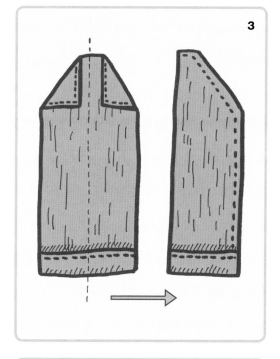

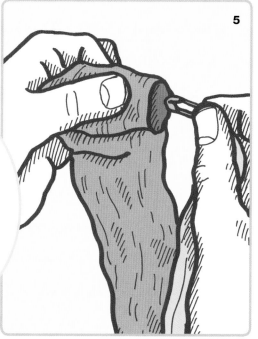

★ ★ ★

Top Tip

Get creative by adding your own adornments and personal touches. If you'd rather be a bit more bullish, why not make the sleeve out of leather?

★ ★ ★

2.11

Jell-O Jerky

Enliven dinner with friends—or perhaps lunch with the in-laws—with Jell-O set in these carefully crafted molds, before you use them for your dirty humping sessions, of course.

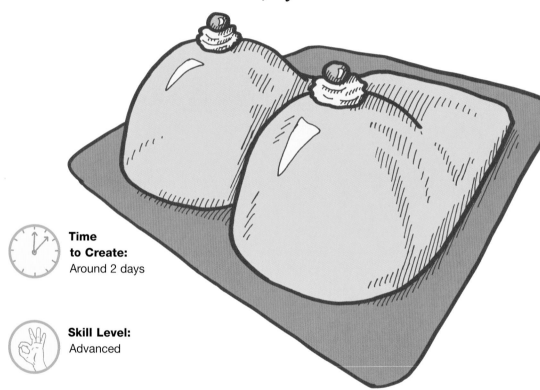

Time to Create:
Around 2 days

Skill Level:
Advanced

You Will Need:
A pair of breasts (or something similar, e.g., two balloons), some Vaseline, a roll or two plaster bandage (available from drug stores, i.e., the same stuff they use to make casts for broken bones), plastic wrap, 1 package of Jell-O, plus decoration ingredients

Mell-O Jell-O
Perhaps better suited to the more sensitive male, these Jell-Os won't take as much of a battering as, say, the Fruity-Scoopy (page 22). Nevertheless, the fleshy sensation is similar, as the jelly wobbles into glorious submission.

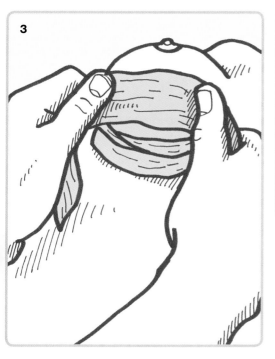

Safety First

Dispose of your waste sensibly, as plaster water can clog your pipes.

Method:

1 Cover the items to be molded with a thin layer of Vaseline, which will make the plaster easier to remove.

2 Cut the plaster bandage into strips. Soak each strip in lukewarm water for a few seconds, then gently squeeze out any excess water, taking care to ensure that it remains as flat as possible.

3 Carefully mold each strip to the breasts (real or improvised). You're aiming to cover them completely, so overlap each strip by about half an inch as you progress. The plaster will begin to set quickly, so work with speed and thoroughness. Apply a second layer for extra strength.

4 Carefully remove the cast and leave it to harden overnight.

5 Line the molds with plastic wrap, trying to avoid any creasing. Prepare the Jell-O according to package instructions. Pour the liquid Jell-O into your mold and leave in the fridge.

6 Once the Jell-O has set, the "breasts" are ready for your consumption. Decorate with nipple-like whipped cream and cherries if you must.

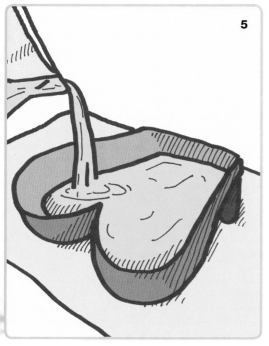

2.12

Crochet Restrictor

These tight (but not too tight) crocheted briefs will have you not only looking good, but feeling great. The restrictive weave ensures you remain harder and stronger for longer.

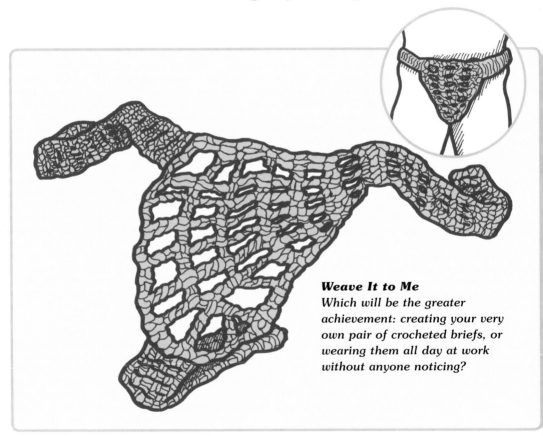

Weave It to Me
Which will be the greater achievement: creating your very own pair of crocheted briefs, or wearing them all day at work without anyone noticing?

Time to Create:
4 hours

Skill Level:
Advanced

You Will Need:
1 crochet hook (size 5.0), 1 ball wool

Method:

For the main triangle:

1 30 stitches for base chain.

2 1 double crochet into the 6th stitch, miss 6 stitches, then double crochet again. Repeat till the end of the chain.

3 Flip the fabric around and make 3 stitches. Add a double crochet stitch into the 3rd stitch.

4 Miss one stitch, then stitch a double crochet.

5 (3rd row) make a double crochet, miss 1 stitch, then double crochet x 5 to the end of the row. (4th row), repeat 3rd row, but double crochet x 4. (5th row) repeat, but double crochet x 5.

For the thong strap:

1 4 stitches for base chain.

2 4 double crochet stitches. Continue the length to the base of the spine, then add another inch.

For the belt:

1 8 stitches for base chain.

2 Crochet 8 stitches and continue to half the length of the waist, then add another inch.

3 Repeat for the second belt.

Upon completion of all crocheting, tie the two belt straps around your waist with as tight a knot as is comfortable. Feed the thong strap up through your butt crack and tie it around the belt straps, again as tight as you like.

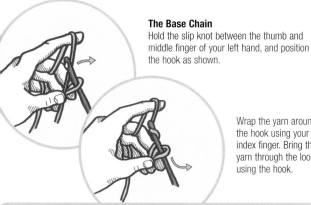

The Base Chain
Hold the slip knot between the thumb and middle finger of your left hand, and position the hook as shown.

Wrap the yarn around the hook using your left index finger. Bring the yarn through the loop using the hook.

To the crochet beginner, this may look very daunting, and it is advisable to find a good introductory book on crocheting from your local library or bookshop in order to learn the basics. Once you're all snug in your restrictor, you'll be so glad you made the effort! And you can put crocheting down as an extra skill on your résumé!

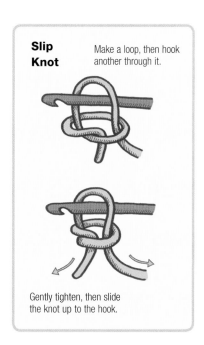

Slip Knot Make a loop, then hook another through it.

Gently tighten, then slide the knot up to the hook.

2.13

Embroidered Embrace

Keep the love flowing from sundown to sunrise as you rest your weary head on pillowcases decorated with stunning erotic designs. They may also prove inspirational if you're not sleeping alone...

Time to Create:
2 hours or more (depending on design)

Skill Level:
Advanced

You Will Need:
1 or more pillowcases, some erotic imagery, access to a photocopier, carbon paper, a pen or pencil, needle, embroidery floss

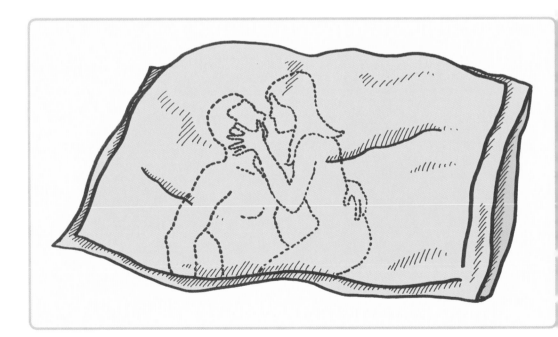

Sweet Dreams
Rest your head on this fine embroidered pillow and the Sandman may very well end up sending you a "special" dream. It's sure to impress any bedfellows, too.

Method:

Choose the kind of imagery you would like to adorn your pillow. A trawl through the Internet or visit to the local library will yield great results. Artists working in this area include Egon Schiele, Henri de Toulouse-Lautrec, and Tom of Finland. You may want to feature icons like Bettie Page, or you can always try drawing your own.

Make a photocopy of the image, correct to the size you wish for your pillow.

Working on a hard surface, copy the image onto the pillow by placing the carbon paper between the photocopy and the fabric and tracing over the outline with a pen or pencil.

Use what's called a *backstitch* to bring the design to life. Bring the thread up through the bottom of the fabric in line with the image outline and then make a small backward stitch through the fabric. Bring the needle up through the fabric again, this time a little in front of the first stitch. Then make another stitch, inserting the needle at the end of the stitch you just made. Your needle will be moving in the opposite direction to your line with each stitch.

Work your way around the outline. Disasters aside, you will be left with a perfect facsimile of your image, rendered in naughty needlework!

* * *

Short Cut

Instead of using carbon paper, heavily shade in the reverse of the photocopy with a pencil. When you come to trace over the outline, the pencil will be transferred onto the fabric perfectly.

* * *

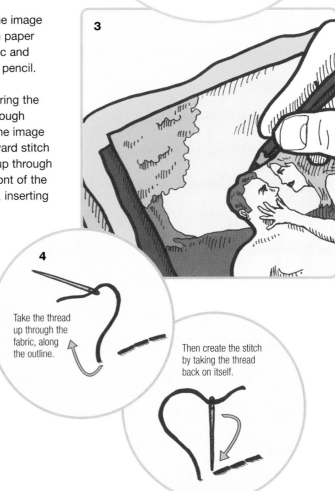

3

4

Take the thread up through the fabric, along the outline.

Then create the stitch by taking the thread back on itself.

2.14

Elastic Extender

The scrotum and its contents are a much-ignored sensual hotspot. Give them the attention they deserve with this basic device that will also give you the low-hangers you've always hankered after.

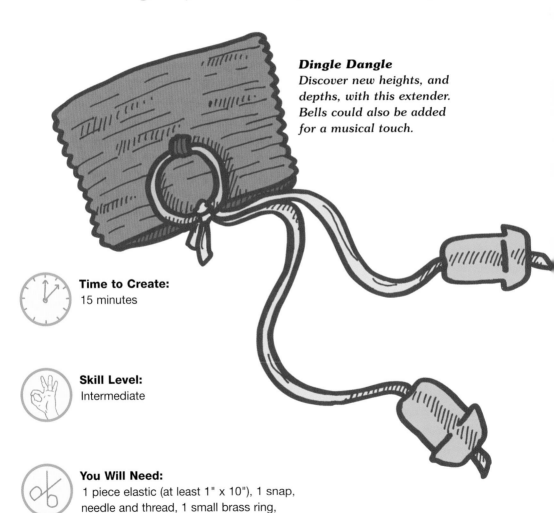

Dingle Dangle
Discover new heights, and depths, with this extender. Bells could also be added for a musical touch.

Time to Create:
15 minutes

Skill Level:
Intermediate

You Will Need:
1 piece elastic (at least 1" x 10"), 1 snap, needle and thread, 1 small brass ring, ribbon or string (at least 10"), 2 weights (e.g., brass pulls for window blinds)

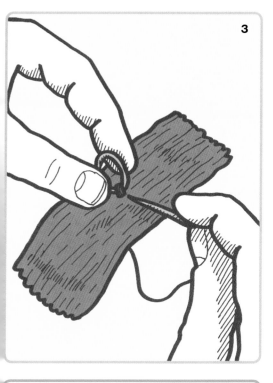

3

Method:

1 Measure your scrotal circumference above, not around, your gonads. Cut a corresponding length of elastic. Hem the ends to avoid fraying.

2 Add one half of the snap fastener to each end, using a needle and thread or a snap-attaching tool.

3 Halfway across, sew on the small brass ring. Then thread through the ring a length of ribbon or string.

4 Finally, attach the brass pulls, or any weighted object of your choice, to the ribbon or string.

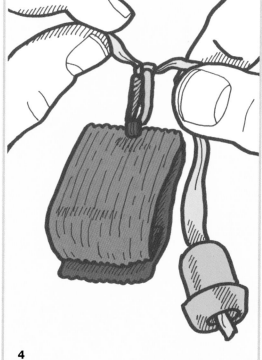

4

Health Warning!

You may be tempted to experiment further. Why not try an old pair of boots, a bag of sugar; heck, why not attach a dumbbell or two? However, remember that with time, gravity will take its course. Do you really want 'nads down to your knees when you're claiming your pension?

2.15

Ribbon Ring

For your partner as much as for yourself, this hoop is decorated with tickling ribbons. It may look like something out of Boy George's wardrobe circa 1982, but rest assured the results are fantastic.

Tie a Yellow Ribbon . . .

. . . *then a blue one, a red one, a green one, and so on. Customize away to enhance pleasure, for both you and your lucky lady.*

Time to Create:
5 minutes

Skill Level:
Beginner

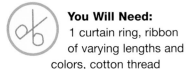

You Will Need:
1 curtain ring, ribbon of varying lengths and colors, cotton thread

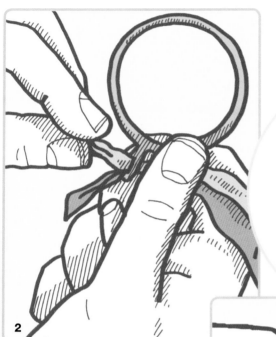

2

Top Tip

Curtain rings come in various finishes and styles. Brass antique ones are particularly attractive.

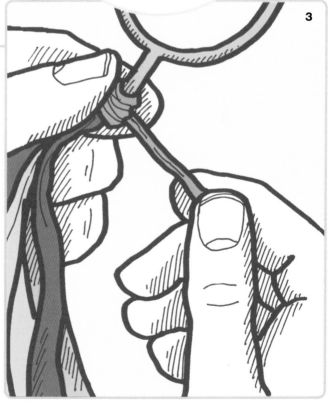

3

Method:

1 Measure your girth correctly using the guide on page 13. Find a curtain ring that will fit snugly around the base of your manhood.

2 Thread three (or more) ribbons through the small hole of the curtain ring.

3 Secure the ribbons by wrapping some cotton thread around them.

4 Tickle away!

For Her

According to Durex's global sex survey, more than one out of every five women has used a vibrator. No need for such expensive outlay anymore, though! Read on...

3.1

Cell Phone Climax

The wonders of modern technology are rich and varied, as amply demonstrated by the good vibrations of a cell phone placed strategically between your legs. One can only wonder what Alexander Graham Bell would make of such uses of his invention.

Time to Create:
1 minute

Skill Level:
Beginner

You Will Need:
1 cell phone with a vibrating function, 1 condom (unlubricated), another phone (optional, depending on the method used)

Good Vibrations
It's estimated that by 2015, four billion people will own a cell phone. That's two out of every three global citizens. And thanks to advances in technology, handsets are getting slimmer and more discreet—perfect for the uses outlined opposite.

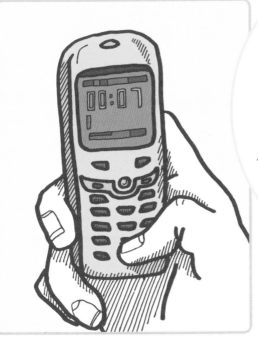

Top Tip

Use a condom, particularly if you are inserting rather than just buzzing it against your panties, and particularly if you want to use the phone again. Cells rarely work with clogged buttons. Also, your cell phone's vibrator motor wears out the battery quickly, so you'll have to recharge it earlier than you normally might.

There are a number of different methods to get you vibrating along with your phone.

Alarm: Set your phone alarm to vibrate however often you want it for however long. One good, regular way is to set it to vibrate every minute.

Alert: The section in your phone that lists different alert functions should allow you to keep it buzzing on vibrate. Keep pressing the select key once you've found the right option. It may take some practice but the effort pays off.

Dualist: Set the phone's ringtone to vibration only, and then call your cell using another phone. The redial button will prove handy if you need more time. Even better, prearrange a partner or close friend to give you a buzz!

3.2

Electro Stimu

Turn it on, turn yourself on. The cell phone is, of course, not the only device that can get you buzzing nicely. If the sound will give your little game away—crank up the radio, sister!

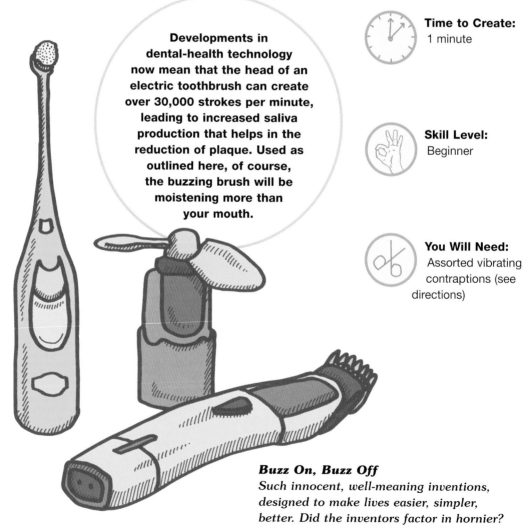

Developments in dental-health technology now mean that the head of an electric toothbrush can create over 30,000 strokes per minute, leading to increased saliva production that helps in the reduction of plaque. Used as outlined here, of course, the buzzing brush will be moistening more than your mouth.

Time to Create:
1 minute

Skill Level:
Beginner

You Will Need:
Assorted vibrating contraptions (see directions)

Buzz On, Buzz Off
Such innocent, well-meaning inventions, designed to make lives easier, simpler, better. Did the inventors factor in hornier?

Electric toothbrush: For such an innocent device, there are many ways in which the electric toothbrush can be used. You may be happy holding the underside against your magic button, or for the more adventurous, why not use the brushes (be mindful of over-abrasion, though)? The handle can also find its own deeper resting place, but make sure you cover it with an unlubricated condom if you think you might insert it. The head can be fitted with a larger, more insertion-friendly object (think hollowed-out cucumber). To avoid the possibility of overnight guests finding short and curly hairs between their incisors, and for other hygiene reasons, wash the toothbrush thoroughly after use or, better yet, designate one for bedroom use and one for bathroom use.

Personal fan, beard trimmer, hair clippers, etc.: Indeed any buzzing, handheld, personal-grooming instrument can be used. Just ensure the handle is covered with an unlubricated condom, and it really cannot be stressed enough that it's the *handle* you want to use. The alternative is too much to think about.

Washer/dryer: Send yourself into a proper spin by carefully perching yourself on the corner of a washing machine or tumble dryer set to the right cycle.

Wiggly-nosed stuffed animals: A more rarefied, but no less satisfying, sensation. If you can find a teddy bear or similar stuffed animal with a vibrating part, he has the power to give you a decidedly adult thrill. Set him off, clasp him to your bare crotch, lie back, and have some R-rated fun.

3.3

Ball Rub

Up, up, and away on your beautiful balloon (or beach ball). Pounce, then bounce, ladies!

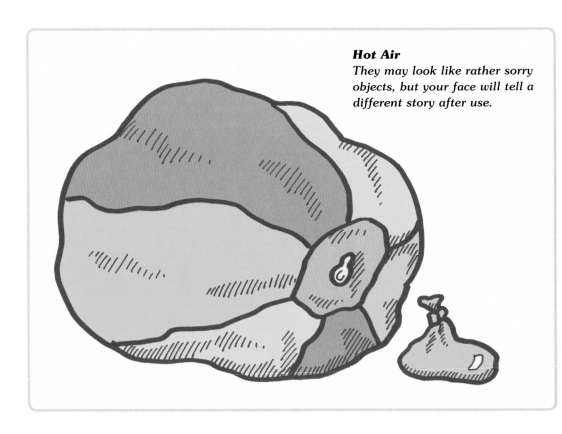

Hot Air
They may look like rather sorry objects, but your face will tell a different story after use.

Time to Create:
5 minutes

Skill Level:
Beginner

You Will Need:
1 balloon and some water, or 1 beach ball

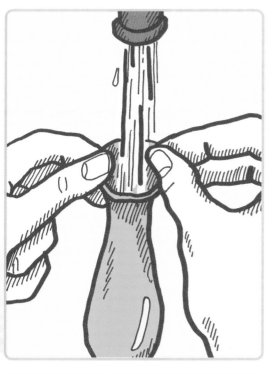

Method:

For the balloon:

1 Fill a regular-sized party balloon with water. Ensure the water is warm (unless you prefer cold), and tie a knot in the end.

2 Apply a coat of water-based lubricant.

3 Rub the balloon against your clitoris for a truly sensual sensation.

For the beach ball:

1 Inflate a small beach ball to about half-capacity.

2 Sit on it! Massage it between your legs, bounce around, let go (mentally) as you ride the ball and it rides you. Mind the nozzle—ouch!

★ ★ ★ ★ ★ ★ ★ ★ ★ ★

Health Warning!

Too much air in the ball or too vigorous an action can cause seams to split and the ball to burst. While this in itself is pretty harmless (even potentially arousing), it may be wise to work it among cushions, in bed, or somewhere with a soft landing space.

★ ★ ★ ★ ★ ★ ★ ★ ★ ★

3.4

Titty-Titty Boom-Boom

Knockers, cans, hooters, headlights—call 'em what you will, but from Pam Anderson to the Pussycat Dolls, boobs always take center stage in the art of the striptease. Dress up your lactation station with some sparkly pasties and shake it like a Polaroid picture!

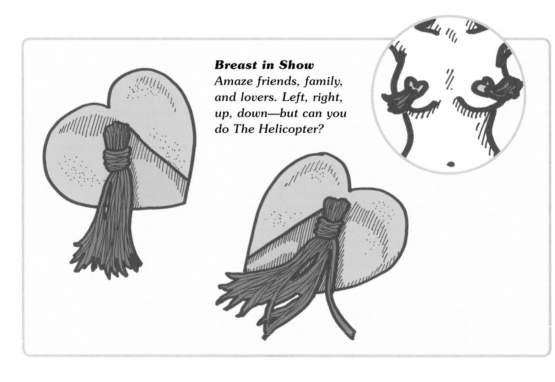

Breast in Show
Amaze friends, family, and lovers. Left, right, up, down—but can you do The Helicopter?

Time to Create:
45 minutes

Skill Level:
Beginner

You Will Need:
Medium-weight card stock, embroidery floss (or similar, at least 45" long), decorative material (e.g., glitter, sequins, feathers, paint), clear double-sided fashion tape ("tit tape"), scissors, glue

Method:

1 Cut out a heart-shape piece of cardstock. Measurements will differ according to your nipple size, but approximately 2" to 3" in diameter will probably do it (experiment with some scrap paper to be certain).

2 Cut a line roughly two-thirds up the middle of the heart. Apply glue to the left side of this incision, then slide the right side on top, carefully bending the card as you go. This will give you a cone shape. Trim off the overhang.

3 For the tassel, cut a long length of embroidery floss (at least 45" long), and fold it 15 times into a bundle roughly 3" long. Sparkly holiday tinsel would also work well here.

4 Pinch about half an inch from the top of the folded floss and take hold of the final bundle. Wrap this excess floss around the top of the bundle several times to secure all the other lengths in place. Draw it around and up through the final loop. Then cut the bottom loops.

5 Decorate the cone with materials of your choice. Once it's dry and ready, poke a small hole through the top. Thread through the spare length of the tassel and secure in place with a knot and/or glue.

6 Repeat steps 1 through 5 to make a second pastie. Finally, use the double-sided tape to attach to your nipples.

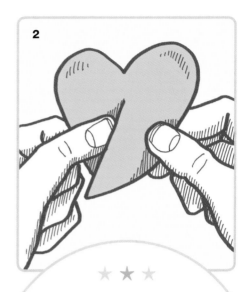

2

★ ★ ★

Fancy That

Ask for a "pastie" in Cornwall, England, and you'll likely be handed a hot pie filled with meat and vegetables. Not so great for boob twirling!

★ ★ ★

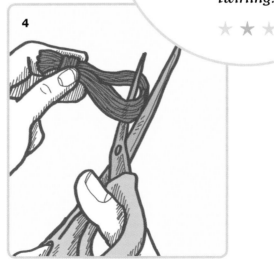

4

3.5

Vegedildo

When hotdogs just won't do (and they probably won't), go veg. If the boys can have melons (see page 22), then surely the girls must have their bananas. Or carrots. Or eggplants. Or...

 **Time to Create:**
1 minute

 Skill Level:
Beginner

You Will Need:
Any phallic vegetable or fruit (see the descriptions for pros and cons of each), condom, lube

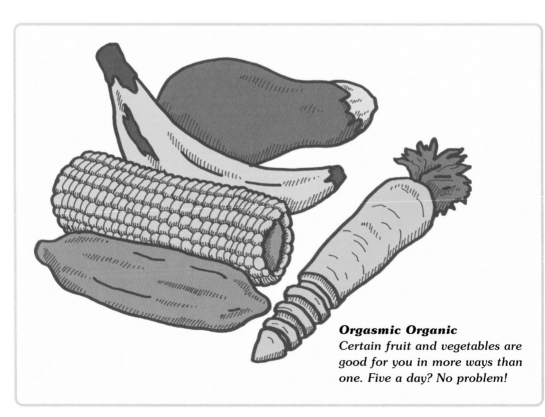

Orgasmic Organic
Certain fruit and vegetables are good for you in more ways than one. Five a day? No problem!

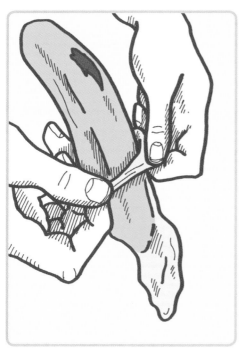

★ ★ ★ ★ ★ ★ ★ ★ ★ ★ ★

Safety Warning

In your haste to have it, don't forget to slide a condom over your produce before insertion!

★ ★ ★ ★ ★ ★ ★ ★ ★ ★ ★

Banana: Native to tropical Southeastern Asia, the banana is usually yellow, though red and green varieties also exist. It should be inserted unpeeled and not too ripe.

Cucumber: The daddy of the vegedildo world is rich in vitamin C, vitamin K, and vitamin O-my-gosh-that's-good. Beginners may want to start with a smaller, thinner variety and work their way up.

Carrot: This root vegetable's hard texture makes it a perfect candidate for some extra shaping and ribbing with a vegetable peeler. Again, though, the beginner should take care not to get too crazy on it.

Eggplant: A prehistoric vegetable that can vary greatly in size. Care must therefore be taken with insertion—too far and too long inside could make for some decidedly rank baba ganoush!

Corn on the cob: Nature's own ribbed dildo, used attentively (narrow end first), should provide you with an arousing session. Remove outer leaves and the long hairy bits before insertion.

Pineapple: Just kidding.

3.6

Wooden Woody

Civilizations have long experimented with penetrative toys (indeed, the word dildo comes from the Latin for "open wide"), and wood was often the traditional material of choice. Here's a little something to help you in your worship of the great god Phallus. Just watch out for the splinters!

Time to Create:
2–3 hours

Skill Level:
Intermediate

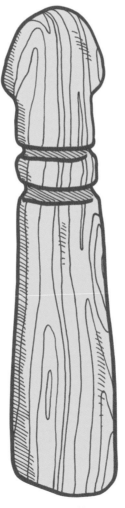

You Will Need:
1 piece wood (many varieties are suitable, e.g., cherry, oak, pine, walnut. No one type is better than the other; it all comes down to aesthetic preference), 1 wood plane, 1 set wood files, a 1/2-round wood rasp, sandpaper (120-grit to 600-grit), wood polish, wood varnish, cloth, condom, lube

Wood Is Good
Standing proud and solid as any timber toy should, the Woody also doubles as a personal safety device.

Easy Does It
To start the molding process, use a wood plane with firm, even-handed strokes.

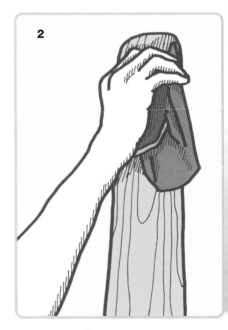

2

Safety Warning

You must ensure that the wood is completely smooth and varnished before use. The tiniest of snags can cause splinters that could prove dangerous and painful.

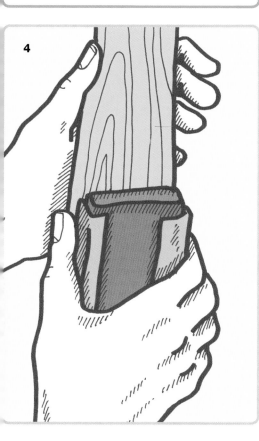

4

Method:

1 Whether you think size matters or not, it certainly will matter when you come to make your own Wooden Woody. From your local lumber yard or hardware store, buy a piece of wood slightly bigger than your desired length and girth—better to have more than less at this stage. Unless you have access to a specialist wood-turning lathe, it's best to start with a ready-rounded piece of wood such as a thick piece of doweling.

2 Having secured it in a vise or similar, work your way over the wood with the plane to round the edges and smooth away any corners. Take your time and work methodically.

3 Smooth the wood further by using a set of files. Going with the grain of the wood, start with the roughest-grade file and progress to the finest. Any indentations, useful for heightened arousal, can be made with the 1/2-round rasp.

4 Sand your Woody as smooth as you can make it. Again use the roughest sandpaper (e.g., 120-grit) first, and end with the finest (400 or 600-grit, used wet). Use light circular motions. Follow with a coat or two of varnish.

5 Hey dildo! Give your new friend a nice buff with the polish and cloth, slip on a condom, and—timber!—meet your own personal lumberjack.

3.7

Willy Candle

An old standby that should leave you waxing lyrical to all your friends about its power. Mind the drips, never light it, and make sure you put it back on the altar when no one's looking.

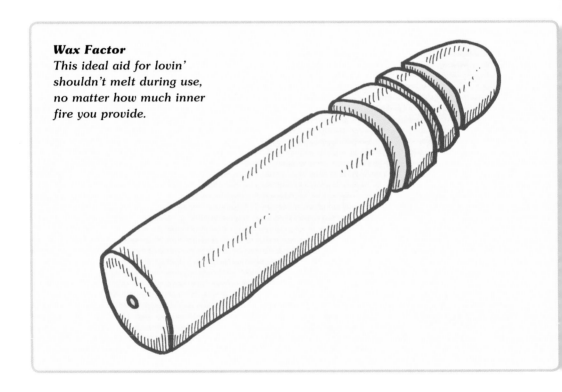

Wax Factor
This ideal aid for lovin' shouldn't melt during use, no matter how much inner fire you provide.

 **Time to Create:**
1 minute

 Skill Level:
Beginner

 You Will Need:
1 candle, condom, lube

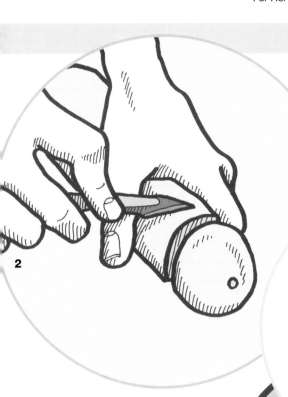

2

Mind Your Fingers
*Adding nicks and
ribbing can be a tricky
business. Always cut
away from the body.*

★ ★ ★

Top Tip

***If you're either very
patient or very bored,
why not try dripping hot
wax into a condom for a
smoother, more phallic
wax wiener?***

★ ★ ★

Method:

1 Choose a candle of appropriate length and girth.

2 If so desired, the candle can be shaped using a sharp craft knife. Extra nicks and ribbing will heighten arousal.

3 Cover with a condom, lube well, and carefully insert. You may like to squeeze and tighten your thighs around the toy to make the sensation even more real.

65

3.8

Love Beads

Not the neckwear favored by the peace and love brigade of the '60s, but a lovingly crafted string of beauties that could soon prove to be your closest friends. They can also be fun at parties: why not find out who among your most intimate friends can "pop" the most?

Time to Create:
10 minutes

Skill Level:
Beginner

You Will Need:
6 or more wooden, ceramic, or plastic beads with stringing holes (each about the size of a marble, available from craft or bead shops), some strong nylon cord (about 12" long), lube

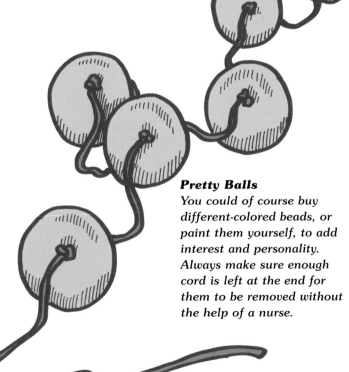

Pretty Balls
You could of course buy different-colored beads, or paint them yourself, to add interest and personality. Always make sure enough cord is left at the end for them to be removed without the help of a nurse.

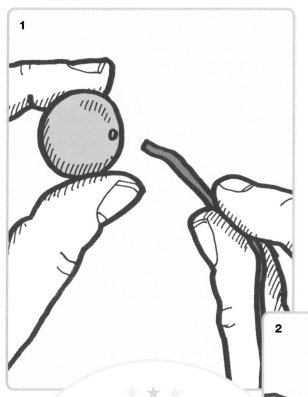

1

2

Method:

1 Thread the cord through one bead.

2 Knot it at both sides and leave about an inch length before progressing to the next.

3 Continue this until a short length of cord is left at one end and, within minutes, your beads will be ready. Lube up and either insert them one by one or run them back to front over your general crotch area. Clean thoroughly before reusing.

★ ★ ★

Top Tip

One nifty trick is to make a version with smaller beads. Then simply sew the cord into your panties and wear them out, in the office, on the factory floor, in the supermarket— maybe not the gym, but you get the idea. A little bit of strokin' gives a whole lotta lovin'!

★ ★ ★

3.9

Leather Strapper

Ping-pong? Ding-dong! Why not liven up a game of table tennis: winner spanks loser? No special equipment needed—just a firm hand!

Time to Create:
10 minutes

Skill Level:
Beginner

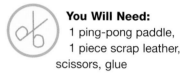

You Will Need:
1 ping-pong paddle,
1 piece scrap leather,
scissors, glue

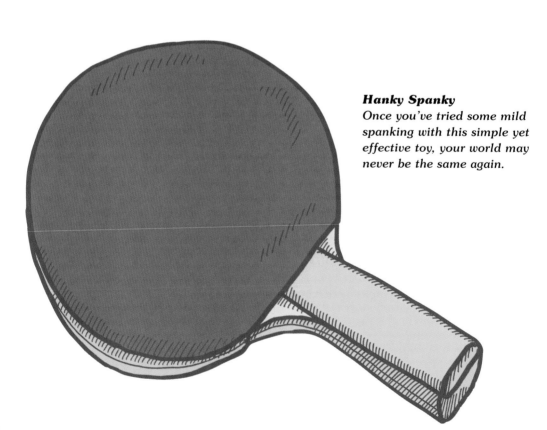

Hanky Spanky
Once you've tried some mild spanking with this simple yet effective toy, your world may never be the same again.

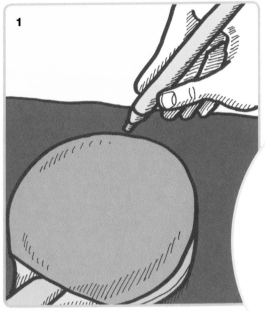

Top Tip

It is advisable to manually massage the relevant area between spanks. Constant beating can result in a deadening of nerve endings and a lessening of the thrill for both spanker and spankee. Regular rubs will ensure the area remains satisfactorily stimulated.

Method:

1 Lie the paddle on top of the leather and draw around its circumference with a marker.

2 Cut around the leather with a sharp pair of scissors.

3 Glue the leather onto the paddle and leave to set.

4 Indulge in a game of hanky-spanky! Administered correctly, the paddle will leave no bruising or welts, just redness and a bit of a sting.

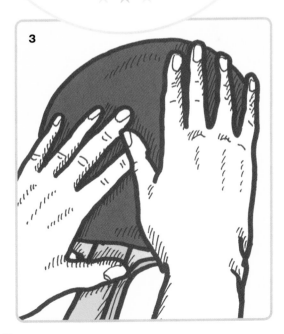

3.10

Pocket in My Panties

Going on a hot date and don't want to take your purse? Where are you going to put the condom? Or maybe you just fancy jazzing up an old pair of panties. This neat underwear-pocket idea is both functional and pretty.

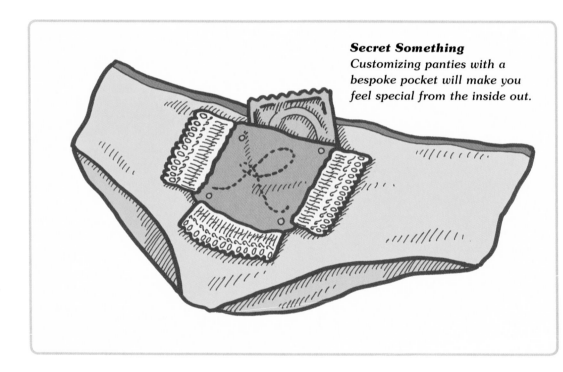

Secret Something
Customizing panties with a bespoke pocket will make you feel special from the inside out.

Time to Create:
30 minutes

Skill Level:
Beginner

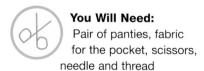

You Will Need:
Pair of panties, fabric for the pocket, scissors, needle and thread

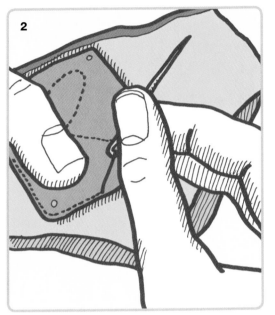

Method:

1 Measure a piece of fabric, 2¹/₂" square. Any decoration of the pocket (such as embroidering your initial) should be done at this stage.

2 Hand sew the pocket onto the knickers using a basic running stitch around three sides. Leave the top open. The pocket can also be placed on the inside, though make sure you leave enough room to completely cover the condom's foil packaging, or uncomfortable chafing may occur.

3 You may also want to add lace trimming around the pocket edge, or other decorations, to personalize your pocket.

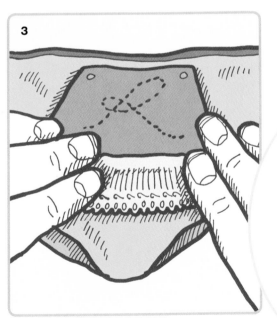

★ ★ ★

Top Tip

Depending on the size of your panties, you may want to increase the size of your pocket. Why not use it to carry items of feminine hygiene, make-up, a little black book, photographs of family and friends...?

★ ★ ★

3.11

The Midas Touch

Old King Midas, according to Greek mythology, was able to turn everything to gold simply by touching it. Your partner, or indeed you, may find it difficult to keep hands off when you cover your boobs with dazzling gold leaf.

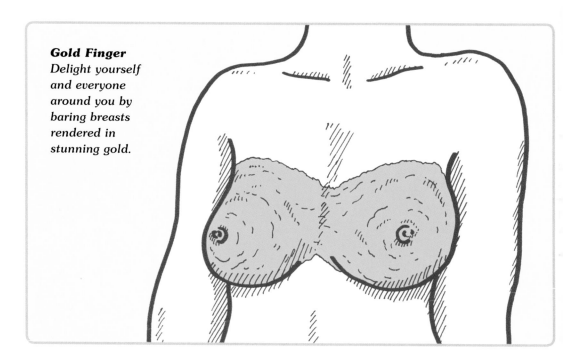

Gold Finger
Delight yourself and everyone around you by baring breasts rendered in stunning gold.

 **Time to Create:**
20 minutes

 Skill Level:
Beginner

You Will Need:
Gold-leaf sheets (inexpensive and available from craft stores), false-eyelash adhesive (a lightweight, nontoxic glue available from drugstores), medium-size brush

Why Not?

You've heard of gilding the lily—why not gild the willy?
Apply the same procedure to the genitals of a willing male
partner and delight in the golden glow (ensure all areas
have been shaved clean before application).

Method:

1 Ensure all areas to be gilded are clean and dry.

2 Apply a layer of false-eyelash adhesive to the area. You don't need too much, but enough to ensure a thorough covering. Perhaps practice on a finger to get the hang of it.

3 Let set for 30 seconds or until tacky.

4 Take one of the gold-leaf sheets and gently apply to the area. Peel off the backing and the results are plain to see. Methodically work over the area to ensure full coverage. You will notice that the gold leaf is delicate and cracks quite easily—you may wish to leave it like that (for a more antique effect), or try and paste more over the cracks.

3.12

Bundled Bunny

For those of you who insist on buying a new-fangled Rabbit Habit vibrator instead of doing-it-yourself (see page 52), this beautiful slipcase will keep your best friend warm, dry, and in tip-top working condition.

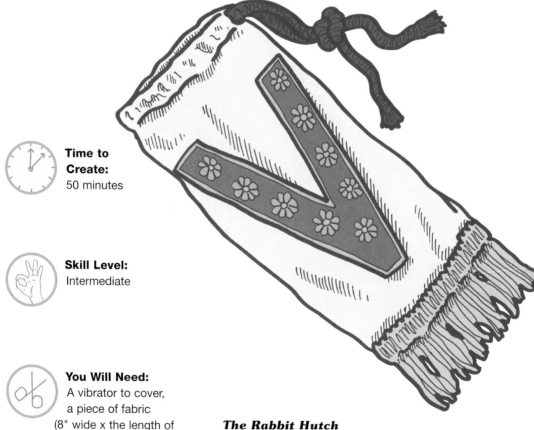

Time to Create:
50 minutes

Skill Level:
Intermediate

You Will Need:
A vibrator to cover, a piece of fabric (8" wide x the length of your vibrator), thick twisted cord, trimming, scissors, glue, needle and thread, see-through sticky tape

The Rabbit Hutch
Stylish and practical, this vibe case won't look out of place in your purse or bathroom. Go to Chapter 5 (pages 113–125) for more storage solutions for your sex toys.

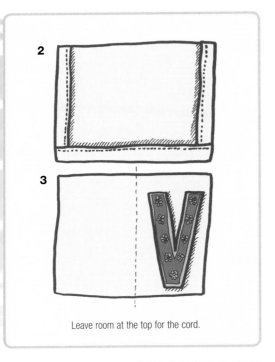

2

3

Leave room at the top for the cord.

Method:

1 Measure your vibrator, then cut a piece of fabric 8" wide by your vibrator's length plus an extra inch.

2 Fold and stitch a 1" hem along all four sides to prevent fraying.

3 Personalize the fabric however you please.

4 Fold the cloth in half lengthwise and close up the bag by stitching along the bottom and side edges.

5 Turn the bag inside out, cut a hole in the top corner, and apply some sticky tape around one of the ends of the twisted cord. Feed the cord through the seam, then remove the tape.

6 Add more decoration, such as trimming along the bottom, and bingo! Bunny's got a home.

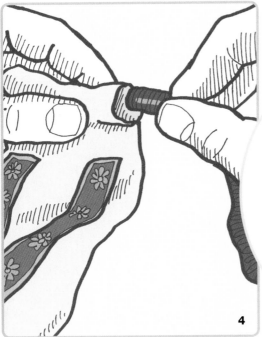

4

★ ★ ★

Top Tip

The example shown here features the owner's initial. You could try adding sequins, beading, or even refer to the erotic embroidery detailed on page 44.

★ ★ ★

Wax Fantastic

Keep as smooth as the day you were born with this marvelous, eco-friendly body-sugaring recipe. Costly trips to the spa may soon become a thing of the past.

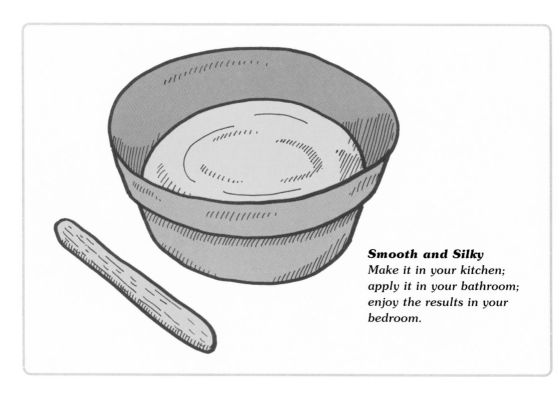

Smooth and Silky
Make it in your kitchen; apply it in your bathroom; enjoy the results in your bedroom.

Time to Create:
15 minutes

Skill Level:
Intermediate

You Will Need:
2 cups sugar, 1/4 cup water, 1/4 cup lemon juice, cornstarch, cotton fabric strips (not too loosely woven), wooden craft stick (to spread the mixture), candy thermometer

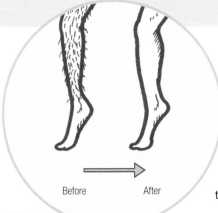

Before   After

Method:

1 Mix together the sugar, water, and lemon juice in a bowl. Transfer to a heavy pot and put over medium heat. Boil gently until the thermometer reads 250°F (120°C). Remove from the heat and let cool to just above body temperature.

2 Ensure the area to be waxed is free of dirt. Lightly dust it with cornstarch. Apply a thin layer of the sugaring solution to the desired area using the craft stick, following the direction of hair growth. The mixture will not work if it is too runny or too tough.

3 Cover with a fabric strip and rub a few times, again in the direction of hair growth.

4 Holding the skin taut, rip off the strip quickly, this time against the direction of hair growth. Repeat for other areas. The mixture can be reheated, either on the stove or in the microwave, but care must be taken not to let it get too hot or boil over.

★ ★ ★

Top Tip

While a DIY Brazilian wax is probably not advisable (best leave it to the experts), why not fashion and style your pubic fuzz into an artistic statement: a heart, star, or even initials? And why not grab your partner and give him a back, sack, and crack wax while you're at it?!

★ ★ ★

The quicker you strip, the less pain you feel.

3.14

Pottery Balls

These love balls can be used day and night, at home, at work, at the bar... anywhere! As well as giving pleasure, they're also very good at strengthening your pelvic-floor muscles. Ball-issimo!

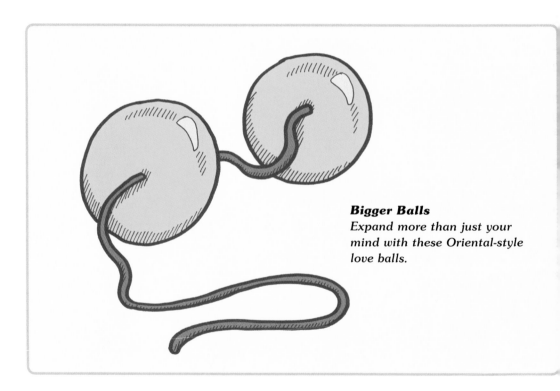

Bigger Balls
Expand more than just your mind with these Oriental-style love balls.

Time to Create:
1 day

Skill Level:
Intermediate

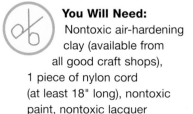

You Will Need:
Nontoxic air-hardening clay (available from all good craft shops), 1 piece of nylon cord (at least 18" long), nontoxic paint, nontoxic lacquer

Method:

1 Cover your chosen work surface with plastic (pieces cut from trash bags work fine) to prevent sticking. With the air clay, roughly mold two ball shapes, about 1" in diameter.

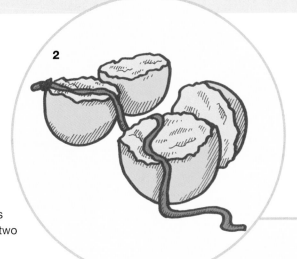

2 Split them in two, and press the nylon cord firmly into the two open tops, leaving about 2" between the balls.

3 Replace the other two halves firmly, then gently remold and reshape the clay into two spheres, taking care not to disturb the cord.

4 Once completed, the balls should be left out in the open for about a day in order for them to harden properly. Any fine adjustment can be made once they are fully dry with a file or sandpaper.

5 Apply nontoxic paint or other decoration to the balls, and then apply a coat of nontoxic lacquer to seal them. You're off!

★ ★ ★ ★ ★ ★ ★ ★ ★ ★ ★ ★ ★ ★ ★ ★ ★ ★ ★ ★

Ancient Balls

These balls are modeled on Ben Wa balls, which originated in Japan around AD 500. Particularly good when used in a rocking chair, any open-minded male acquaintance may also find his own uses for them.

★ ★ ★ ★ ★ ★ ★ ★ ★ ★ ★ ★ ★ ★ ★ ★ ★ ★ ★ ★

3.15

Lacy Lady

The history of lace-making is rich and varied, spanning many centuries and numerous countries. Evoke some of its charm and grace by making and wearing this deluxe lace thong.

Time to Create:
45 minutes

Skill Level:
Beginner

You Will Need:
Lace (at least 26" x 1½"), 3 pieces of ribbon (each at least 9" long), needle and thread, scissors

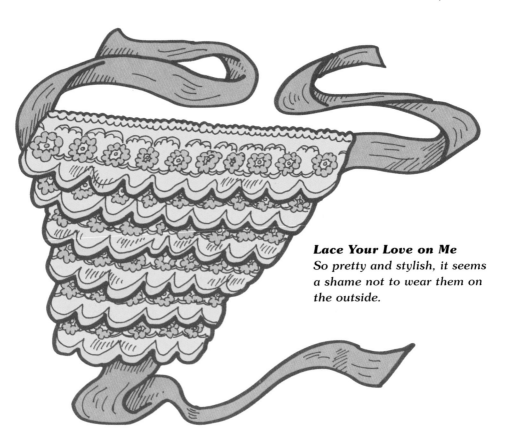

Lace Your Love on Me
So pretty and stylish, it seems a shame not to wear them on the outside.

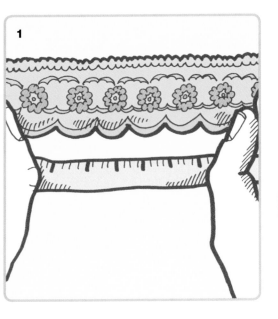

Top Tip

Why not try using different-colored threads to add interest to your thong?

Method:

1 Measure along your pubic bone the desired length of the top of the thong and cut a corresponding length of lace.

2 Cut another length of lace, reducing its length by half an inch. Sew this piece underneath the first, overlapping by about half the width.

3 Continue measuring, cutting, and sewing pieces of lace, each one half an inch shorter and sewn underneath the previous one. You should eventually be left with a triangle that covers your pubic area to a satisfying degree of skimpiness.

4 Attach a ribbon to each side of the top of the lace triangle, and one to the bottom (which will feed up and through the butt crack). Tie all in place and do your thong!

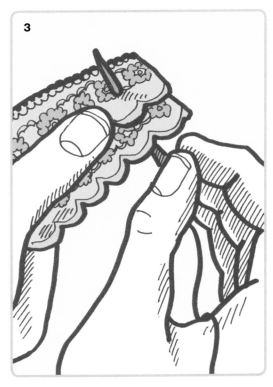

For Couples

So far it's all been a bit lonesome,

but now it's time to tango.

Chocolate body paint, crocheted

gimp masks, strap-on salamis, and

more—it's all waiting . . .

4.1

Positions Quilt

Similar to the Embroidered Embrace (page 44), this piece of patchwork will keep you warm and inspired, especially for when the nights get colder and longer.

Sleep Tight
A good night in bed is guaranteed under this quilt. Interpret that how you wish . . .

Time to Create:
Depends on the desired size

Skill Level:
Intermediate

You Will Need:
Fabric (roughly 4 yards of odd scraps and remnants for the top and 4 solid yards for the backing), felt (optional), scissors, needle and thread, iron

Method:

1 Measure and cut out a 6" x 6" piece of fabric for one patchwork square.

2 Either embroider a sexy image onto the square or cut out a sexy shape in felt and sew it on.

3 Complete as many squares as you want using the method above. Arrange them into the patchwork pattern you want for your quilt.

4 To make the quilt, take two completed fabric squares. Place one facedown directly over the other, so that the finished sides are touching. Sew along the length of one edge using small, neat stitches. Continue by adding more squares and sewing the necessary edges together.

5 When you've finished sewing all the squares together, iron all the seams flat. Stitch on the fabric backing and your kinky quilt is ready for stuffing!

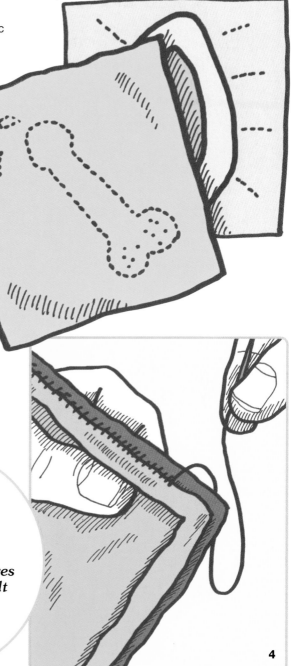

★ ★ ★

Short Cut

*Simply enlarge
the size of the squares
if you want the quilt
done faster.*

★ ★ ★

4

4.2

Chocolate Body Paint

Suitable for even the pickiest eaters, this chocolate paint will provide hours of fun for both of you. Spit or swallow? Go on—swallow!

 Time to Create: 10 minutes

 Skill Level: Beginner

You Will Need: 1 saucepan, water, 1 Pyrex bowl, 4 oz chocolate chips (plain, milk, or white—the choice is yours entirely), 4 oz butter, 1 paintbrush (optional)

The Chocolate Factory
This easy recipe will provide the kind of enjoyment Willy Wonka could only dream of.

Method:

1 Fill the saucepan halfway with water and bring to a low boil. Then balance the bowl containing the chocolate chips and butter on top of the saucepan.

2 Stir slowly as the chocolate and butter melt.

3 Voila! In a matter of minutes, the gooey mixture is ready for application. Let the mixture cool to a comfortable temperature. Use the brush (if desired) for more artistic applications, or just dab your loved one with the end of your finger (or any other appendage you may think of).

Chocolate Pioneers

The first tribes to discover culinary uses for the seeds from cacao trees were found in the tropical rainforests of the Americas more than 2,000 years ago. Americans now consume more than 3.1 billion pounds of it every year, most of it from a wrapper rather than each other.

Duo Ring

So all the rings and things featured in the guys' section earlier are all very well and good, but with this one simple addition, both of you can enjoy a new level of satisfaction and pleasure.

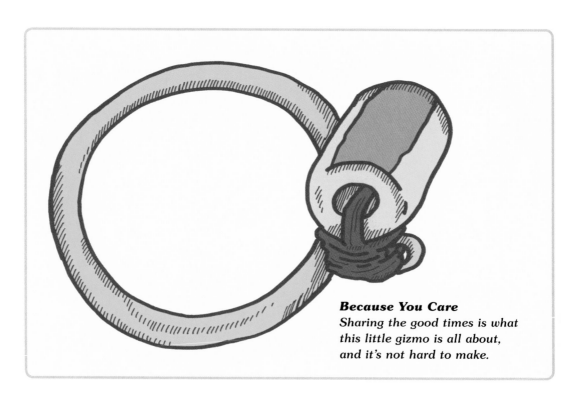

Because You Care
Sharing the good times is what this little gizmo is all about, and it's not hard to make.

Time to Create:
5 minutes

Skill Level:
Beginner

You Will Need:
1 curtain ring, 1 bead, nylon string

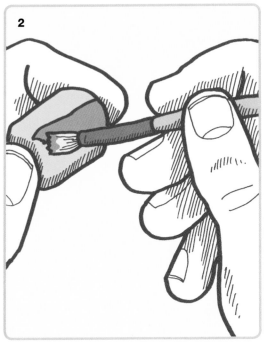

Safety First!

Too tight a cockring can result in a very unpleasant condition known as priapism— i.e., never-ending penile engorgement. This can get quite serious, leading to gangrene and genital loss, so do measure up correctly and always err on the side of caution.

Method:

1 Ensure you use the right-size ring by following the girth measurement advice on page 13.

2 Find a large bead with a stringing hole: wooden ones are very handy (such as the ones from old car seat covers), or a plastic one can be equally effective. You may want to decorate the bead at this point.

3 Thread the string through both the bead and the ring's smaller hole to bind the two together.

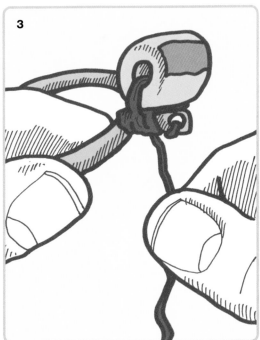

4.4

Mutual Member

So many holes, so little time! Discover each other's ins and outs with this multifaceted double-dildo!

Time to Create:
1 day

Skill Level:
Intermediate

You Will Need:
Nontoxic air-hardening clay (available from good craft shops) or similar, nontoxic paint (optional), non-toxic lacquer, condom, lube

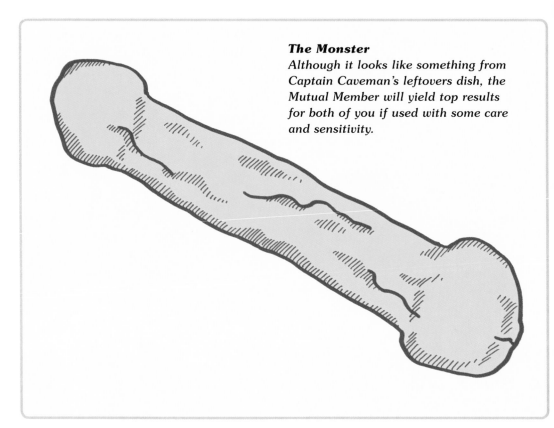

The Monster
Although it looks like something from Captain Caveman's leftovers dish, the Mutual Member will yield top results for both of you if used with some care and sensitivity.

Method:

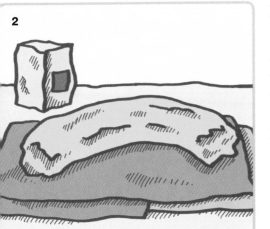

1 Work out together what exactly you *both* want from the Mutual Member. Small bumps added to the main shaft, for example, may improve stimulation for her.

2 To prevent sticking, cover your work surface with plastic. Roll out the clay and mold into the desired shape.

3 Leave to dry in the open for about a day. Once hard, you may want to make it truly yours by decorating the Member with a spot of nontoxic paint decoration. Apply a coat of sealing lacquer, a condom, and some lube before use.

★ ★

G-Spotting

Far from being the sole preserve of women, men do indeed have their own internal magic button. The prostate gland is located at the front of the rectum and, when massaged, can release a whole new world of pleasure and satisfaction. It's even possible to come without touching any other part of your body.

★ ★

4.5

Hardware Hardcore

With a little imagination, even the most innocent of objects can assume new roles. Here is just a hint of what can be done with a trip down to the local hardware store.

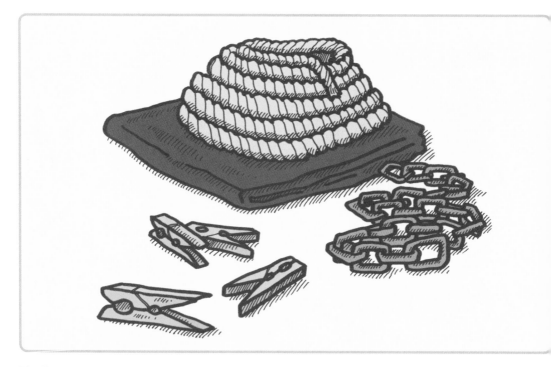

No Pain, No Gain
Rope, trash bags, chains, and clothespins are just some of the items widely available and easily adapted for your bedroom/dungeon.

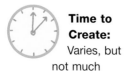 **Time to Create:** Varies, but not much

 Skill Level: Beginner

 You Will Need: Imagination, a hardware store

Clothespin Tit Clamps: Pinned onto sensitive areas of the body, both men and women can feel the pull of the pinch at a very low cost with simple clothespins. Chaining up a pair and clipping them onto the nipples can make for some highly fulfilling edge-play. A word to the wise: Brand-new clothespins will clamp very tightly! For advanced players only.

Tie Me Up, Tie Me Down: Stores are full of restraint devices. Think padlocks, heavy-duty rope, garden chains, garden twine, bungee cords, electrical cabling . . .

Rubbered Up: By carefully cutting up industrial-strength black trash bags, you can make yourself some very effective yet very economical rubber-like sheets.

The term "S&M" (sadomasochism) is usually used to describe safe, sane consensual acts between two adults that incorporate some elements of control, domination, or pain exchange. Here, it also stands for Saving Money.

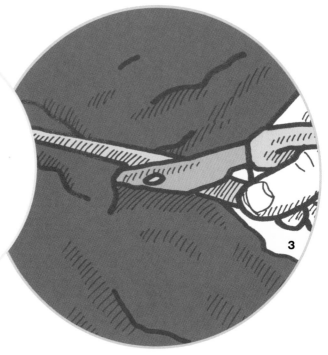

4.6

James Bondage

Otherwise known as "the spy who got tied up."
Have fun with your lover by customizing old clothing—
you'll never say never again.

Time to Create:
20 minutes

Skill Level:
Beginner

You Will Need:
1 old tuxedo, needle and thread

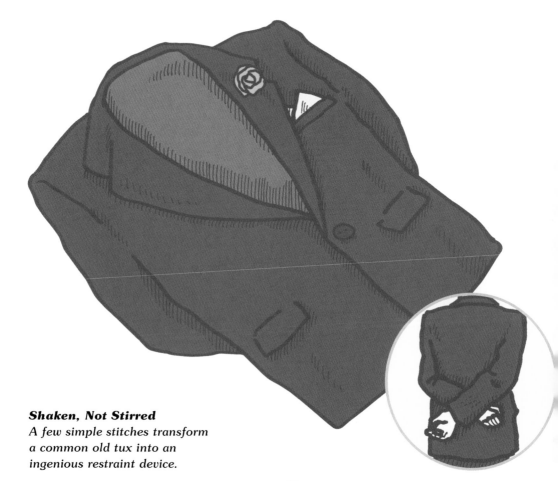

Shaken, Not Stirred
A few simple stitches transform
a common old tux into an
ingenious restraint device.

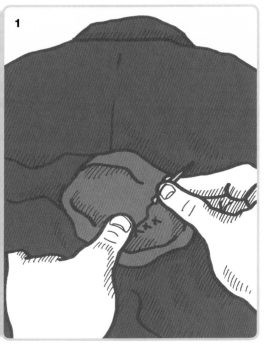

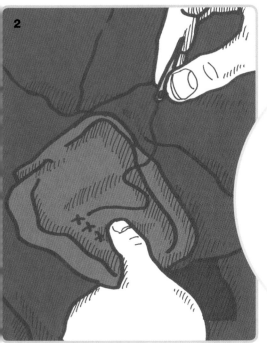

Method:

1 Take the left arm of the jacket and sew it to the back with a series of strong stitches. Remember that the "victim" will need to put their hands through the arms of the jacket, so only sew the side of the cuff nearest the back.

2 Now place the right arm in a suitable place over the top of the left one. Again using strong stitches, sew it in place.

3 When the "victim" puts on the jacket, ensure their arms are comfortable enough (but not too comfortable). Button up the jacket front. For extra security, you may want to consider tying leather belts, rope, or heavy-duty bungee cords around their body too.

★ ★ ★

Top Tip

Why not make an evening of it by hosting a bondage banquet, complete with forced feeding, teasing, and other inspired naughtiness? And if one of you gets bored, change jackets.

★ ★ ★

4.7

Cat-o'-However-Many-Tails-You-Want

Whip-crack-away! Take Michelle Pfeiffer's catsuit as your inspiration for this simple-to-make, easy-to-use whip with added extras.

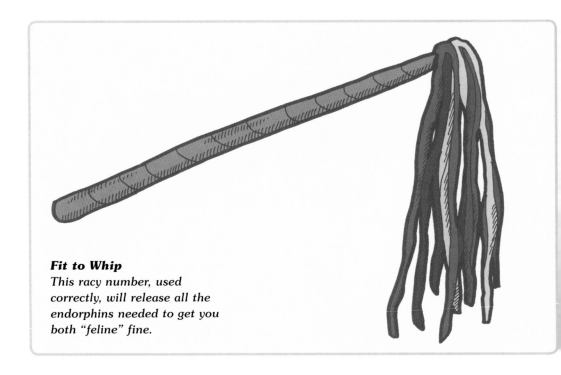

Fit to Whip
This racy number, used correctly, will release all the endorphins needed to get you both "feline" fine.

 **Time to Create:**
1 hour

 Skill Level:
Beginner

You Will Need:
1 long, flexible stick (easy to find at local hardware or garden supply stores), black leather shoelaces, black duct tape

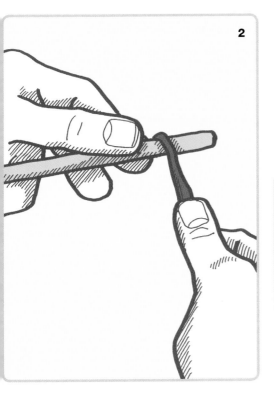

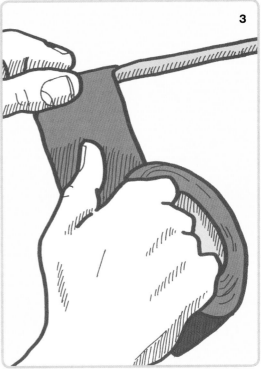

Method:

1 Ensure the stick is flexible and sturdy enough to whip.

2 Gather together the required number of "tails" (i.e., the shoelaces) and wind them once or twice around the top of the stick.

3 Attach the laces to the stick by winding the duct tape around them, and continue winding the tape around the stick until it is completely covered.

4 Meow! Whip your loved one into shape with this pussy whip, and if they get a bit mouthy, you can always plaster a bit of duct tape over their sniveling little mouth.

4.8

Lotions & Potions

For a more sensuous and gentle night in, concoct some inspirational massage lotions to soothe and excite both you and your partner.

★ ★ ★ ★ ★ ★ ★ Fancy That! ★ ★ ★ ★ ★ ★ ★

When applied to the skin, essential oils act upon thermal receptors and can kill microbes and fungi. Aromatherapy was first "discovered" by French scientist René-Maurice Gattefosse. Working in his laboratory in the 1920s, he accidentally set his arm on fire and plunged it into the first vat of cold liquid he could find. This vat contained lavender oil, and Gattefosse was amazed to discover the wound healed quickly and with little scarring.

Time to Create:
10 minutes

Skill Level:
Beginner

You Will Need:
1 glass bottle, 6–8 tsp carrier oil, 8 drops essential oil (see box for examples)

2

3

Method:

1 Ensure the glass bottle is completely clean and dry.

2 Combine the carrier oil with the essential oil in the bottle.

3 Massage gently into your partner's skin.

4 Any leftover oil can be stored in the bottle, providing it has a tight-fitting lid.

Sensual Suggestions

Light carrier oils are best: recommended are sweet almond, apricot kernel, grapeseed, canola, safflower, sunflower, sesame, wheat germ, olive, groundnut, or peanut oil. Mind your partner's allergies, if any. Essential oils known for their euphoric or sensual scents include jasmine, rosewood, ylang-ylang, sandalwood, ginger, patchouli, and grapefruit.

Example 1—for him:
Combine 6 to 8 teaspoons sunflower oil with 2 drops ylang-ylang, 2 drops sandalwood, and 6 drops frankincense.

Example 2—for her:
Combine 6 to 8 teaspoons sunflower oil with 1 drop geranium, 2 drops rosewood, 2 drops grapefruit, and 3 drops bergamot.

4.9

Silk Blindfold

They say that "love is blind," and it sure will be once you get this fetching and arousing blindfold around your mate's head.

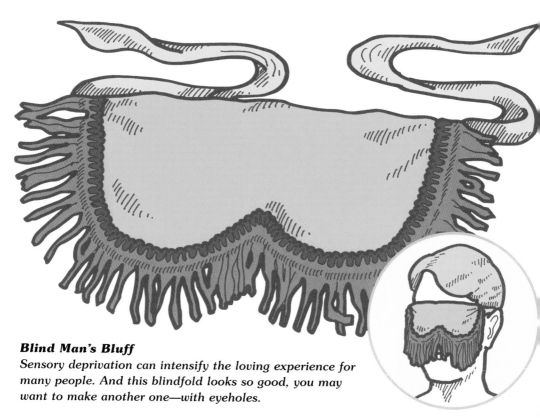

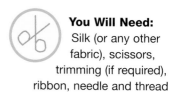

Blind Man's Bluff
Sensory deprivation can intensify the loving experience for many people. And this blindfold looks so good, you may want to make another one—with eyeholes.

Time to Create:
20 minutes

Skill Level:
Intermediate

You Will Need:
Silk (or any other fabric), scissors, trimming (if required), ribbon, needle and thread

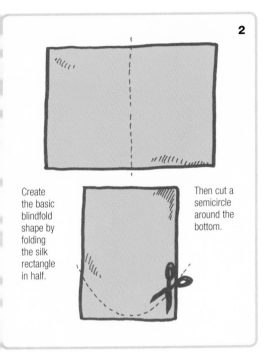

2

Create the basic blindfold shape by folding the silk rectangle in half.

Then cut a semicircle around the bottom.

Method:

1 Measure the width of your, or your partner's, face, temple to temple. Cut a rectangle of silk to that length, and roughly 4" deep.

2 Fold that in half and mark a semicircle that goes round the bottom. Cut round the semicircle.

3 If you're adding trimming or other decorations to the blindfold, do it now.

4 Then cut two lengths of ribbon long enough to tie the blindfold at the back of the head. Hem each end and sew onto the corners of the blindfold.

5 Tie firmly around your head or that of your lover. Ensure it is tight enough—and no peeking!

4

★ ★ ★

Budget Option

For a cheaper, more urban look, take a pair of industrial goggles (available from hardware stores). Ensure they have seals around the eyes to limit the vision properly, and spray the lenses black with spray paint. Once dry, wear them with pride (or fear— whichever you prefer).

★ ★ ★

4.10

Leather Leash

When Iggy Pop sang "I Wanna Be Your Dog" in 1968, chances are he wanted to fit a leash such as this around his taut little neck. For maximum pleasure, this could be used in conjunction with the Crochet Collar (pages 104–105).

Time to Create:
15 minutes

Woof, Woof!
A fine toy for both to enjoy.
It could even be used in public,
if you like that kind of thing.

Skill Level:
Beginner (if you know how to braid)

You Will Need:
9 long leather laces (or more, depending on how loose a leash you like)

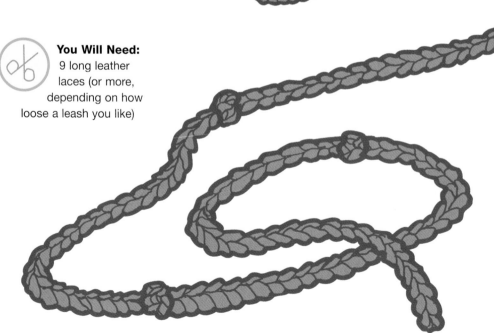

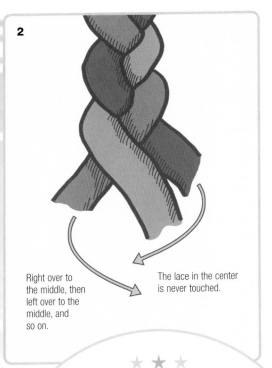

2

Right over to the middle, then left over to the middle, and so on.

The lace in the center is never touched.

Method:

1 Divide the laces into three lots of three.

2 Lay three next to each other. Take the lace on the right and pass it over to the middle. Then take the lace on the left and pass it over to the middle. The middle lace is never handled—it's just the left and right ones moving in to take their place in the middle according to their turn.

3 Do the same for the other two sets of three laces.

4 Tie each set to the next with a secure knot. There should be enough left over to slip around your hand, and attach securely to your hound's collar. Make more if needed.

★ ★ ★

Fancy That

Iggy Pop is considered by many to be the Grandfather of Punk. Early concerts saw him smearing himself with raw meat and peanut butter, cutting himself with broken bottles, and pioneering the stage-dive. If he had indeed been put on a leash, the story of rock 'n' roll may have been very, very different.

★ ★ ★

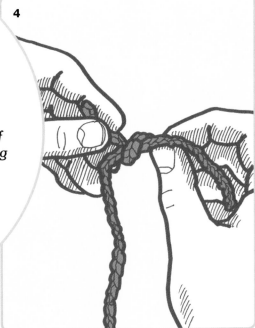

4

4.11

Crochet Collar

The perfect accompaniment to the Leather Leash (previous page), this collar will have you begging for more from your respective master or mistress.

 Time to Create: 1 hour

 Skill Level: Advanced

 You Will Need: 1 crochet hook (size 5.0), 1 ball of wool, 1 button, 1 brass ring, needle and thread

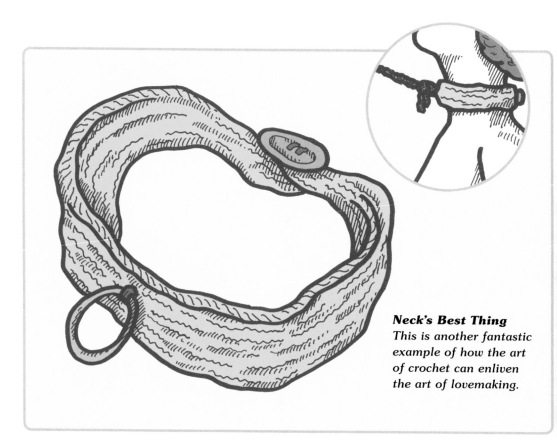

Neck's Best Thing
This is another fantastic example of how the art of crochet can enliven the art of lovemaking.

Method:

1 Crochet 55 chain stitches.

2 Crochet single stitch all along. Then flip fabric over and repeat for 6 rows.

3 At the end of the strip, crochet 2 stitches in. Then 6 stitches and connect chain to the stitches on the other side. This is your button loop.

4 Continue to crochet down that side to the end to finish off the edges neatly.

5 Sew on the button at the other end.

6 Sew on the brass ring in the middle of the collar.

7 Attach the leash and it's time for a w-a-l-k.

The base chain after making five stitches . . .

. . . And this is it from the back.

Those not familiar with crochet may find it helpful to refer to a beginner's book on the subject.

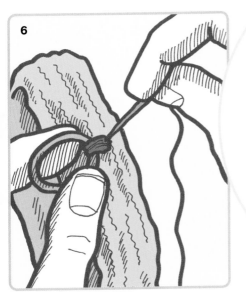

6

★ ★ ★

Top Tip

Given how darned BEAUTIFUL this toy looks, no one would think twice if a woman were to choose to wear it to the mall, running errands, or lounging around the house, particularly if customized with a carefully chosen scarf or bandana. If you do wear it to your local restaurant, however, remember not to ask for your food in a dogbowl.

★ ★ ★

4.12

Gimp Mask

"Bring out the gimp." So says Zed, a character from Quentin Tarantino's Pulp Fiction. Why not re-create that seminal piece of movie history in the comfort of your own home with this delightful, unisex, knitted gimp mask?

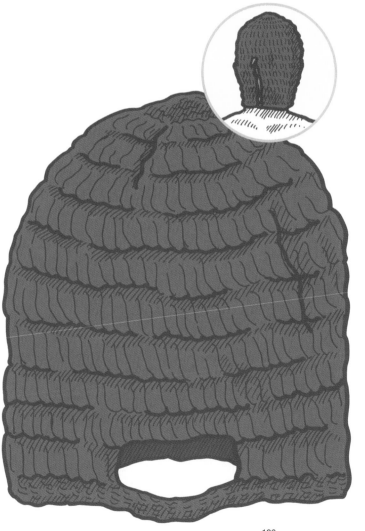

Time to Create:
2 days

Skill Level:
Advanced

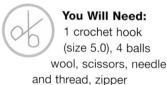

You Will Need:
1 crochet hook (size 5.0), 4 balls wool, scissors, needle and thread, zipper

Help the Aged
This mask is very warm and cozy. Why not lend it to an elderly relative during the cold winter months?

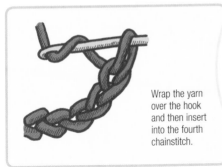

Wrap the yarn over the hook and then insert into the fourth chainstitch.

Yarn over, pull through and yarn over again, so there are four loops still on the hook.

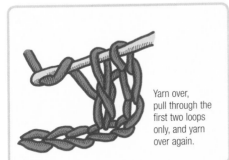

Yarn over, pull through the first two loops only, and yarn over again.

Pull through the last two loops on the hook.

★ ★ ★

Top Tip

When your mask needs a wash, do it by hand in cold water. A blast in the washing machine will reduce it to a shrunken mess.

★ ★ ★

The four step-by-step illustrations, left, show you how to make a treble stitch.

Method:

1 Crochet base chain, casting on 7 and connecting ends to make a circle.

2 Add 2 stitches onto each stitch until the base circle is approx 3" in diameter.

3 2 treble stitches in each stitch (1st row).

4 1 treble stitch in each stitch (2nd row).

5 1 treble stitch in each stitch (3rd row).

6 1 treble stitch, then a treble x 2 every other stitch. This will expand the fabric.

7 1 treble every other stitch.

8 Crochet a treble stitch and leave a gap at the end of the row for the zip.

9 Continue stage 8 until the mouth.

10 Reduce stitches and cast off.

11 Sew in zipper. Away you go. For ultimate sensory deprivation, why not tie on the Silk Blindfold (page 100) before masking up your gimp. And shove an orange in its mouth. And cheese in its ears.

4.13

Strap-On Salami

Or the Strap-On Salad for vegetarians. No right-thinking DIY sex-toy player's kit will be without this beauty—a model of finesse, ingenuity, and affordability. Were there Olympics for homemade sex toys, this toy would take gold.

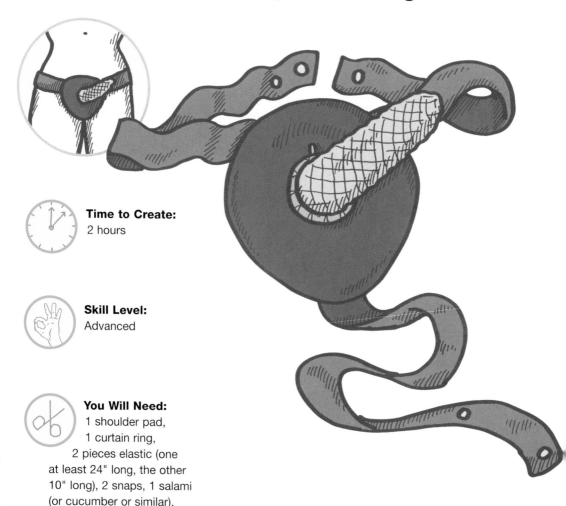

Time to Create:
2 hours

Skill Level:
Advanced

You Will Need:
1 shoulder pad,
1 curtain ring,
2 pieces elastic (one
at least 24" long, the other
10" long), 2 snaps, 1 salami
(or cucumber or similar),
varnish, condom, lube

Method:

1 Is this toy to be used by both of you or just one? For two, ensure the larger person's measurements are the ones followed—allowances are made for the smaller partner with optional additional snaps.

2 Measure your hips and cut a corresponding length of the elastic. It needs to be quite tight, though obviously some room must be left for blood flow. Attach a snap to each end (and one for your partner's measurements if required).

3 Take the shoulder pad and cut a hole (the same diameter of the curtain ring) through the middle. Sew the ring to the hole, then attach the top of the pad to the center of the hip-band elastic with secure stitches.

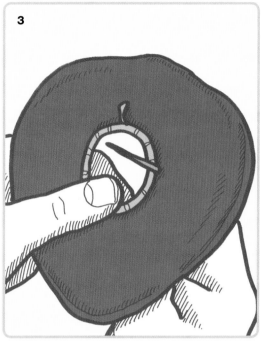

3

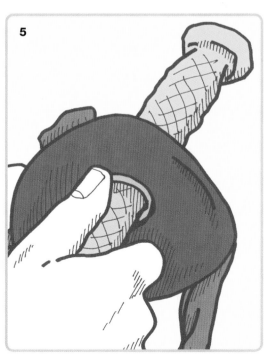

5

4 Sew the second strap of elastic (the one that goes up round your butt crack) to the bottom of the pad and attach snaps to the other end (so you can loop it over the hip band).

5 Pick your phallus of choice, which must fit through the curtain ring. Ensure the base is thicker than the shaft (you'll need to do some careful carving). Seal it with varnish, cover it with a condom, and lube it up before insertion.

6 You're off! You may need some practice, and plenty of lube for each orifice, but used carefully and skillfully, you should enjoy hours of fun.

4.14

Shawl Thing

The perfect accompaniment to the post-DIY-sex-toy coital comedown: a heart-emblazoned shawl for cuddling up to your partner as you whisper sweet nothings and try to get the glue off your hands.

Time to Create:
1–2 days

Skill Level:
Advanced

You Will Need:
1 crochet hook (size 5.0), 2–5 balls of wool (depending how big you want it), needle and thread, scissors

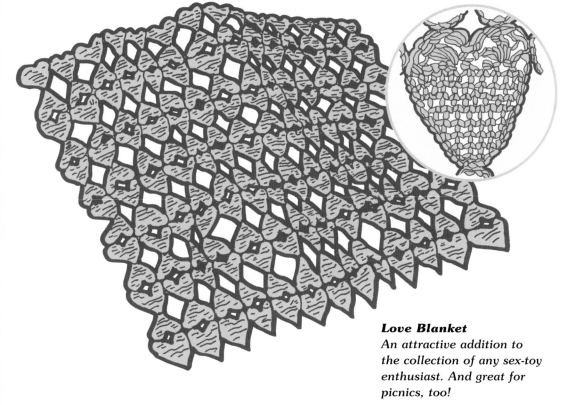

Love Blanket
An attractive addition to the collection of any sex-toy enthusiast. And great for picnics, too!

Insert the hook into the first stitch.

Wrap the yarn over.

Pull up a loop so you have 2 loops on the hook.

Yarn over again, and draw through both loops on the hook.

★ ★ ★

Fancy That

The heart-shaped icon has long been used to denote love, though its resemblance to the actual human heart is negligible. Some have suggested it more closely resembles, among other things, the shape of a cow's heart, a turtle's heart, a woman's pubic region, a woman's breasts, or the male prostate gland.

★ ★ ★

Method:

1 Crochet base chain, 5 stitches.

2 Crochet single stitches (2nd and 3rd row).

3 Add extra stitch (4th row).

4 Increase by 1 stitch and crochet a row (5th row).

5 Increase by 2 stitches and crochet a row (6th row). Your fabric should now be fanning outwards. By row 12, there should be at least 12 stitches.

6 Miss 3 stitches and crochet 4 treble clusters in the 4th stitch.

7 Pull fan shape with 1 stitch to center of fabric.

8 Skip 2 stitches, repeat stage 6—now you have the top of your heart.

Continue to crochet different heart shapes, sewing them together as you go, to make as big a shawl as you want.

The four step-by-step illustrations, left, show you how to make a single crochet stitch.

Storage and Organizers

Now that you've made your toys and had a whole lotta fun using them, one question remains: where to keep them all?

5.1

Bedside Tidy

This ingenious device solves two problems: where to store the smaller toys in your collection, and what to do with used, leftover toilet-paper rolls.

Time to Create:
30 minutes

Skill Level:
Beginner

You Will Need:
Assorted toilet-paper and paper-towel rolls, cardboard, paint or contact paper, glue, craft knife

Roll Up
You might have made one of these as a kid, but this crafty version is definitely the R-rated model. Just as functional, though.

2

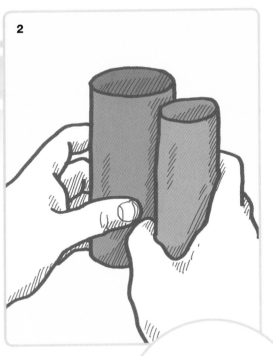

Method:

1 Paint your rolls, or you may want to cover them in contact paper.

2 Once dry, arrange them in the order in which you'd like them, and then glue them together.

3 Sit the Bedside Tidy onto the piece of cardboard and draw around the base. Then cut the shape out of the cardboard with the craft knife. Glue the rolls onto the base.

Presto!

Your small toys are nice and orderly, and within reach when the mood strikes you.

3

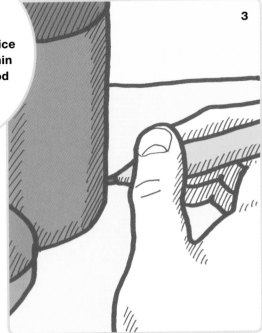

Nice and Easy
With a few swipes of a knife and a few swabs of glue, you have a perfect storage solution. There's nothing to stop you adding more rolls as your collection gets bigger.

5.2

Saddle Bag

A simple belt-and-pocket combo that will keep your toys close at hand. It's portable, too—perfect for people on the move. Saddle up and ride 'em home!

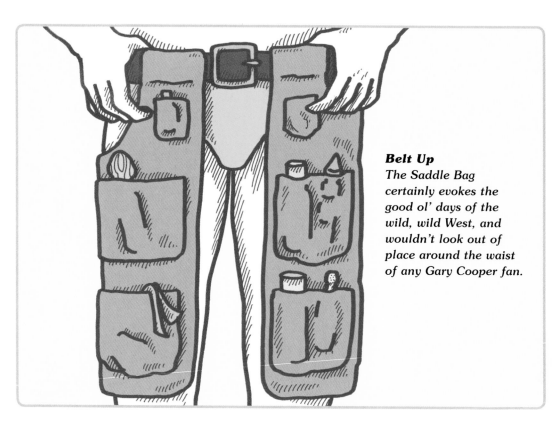

Belt Up

The Saddle Bag certainly evokes the good ol' days of the wild, wild West, and wouldn't look out of place around the waist of any Gary Cooper fan.

Time to Create:
45 minutes

Skill Level:
Intermediate

You Will Need:
1 belt, 2 large pieces of felt, more felt for the pockets (you may want different colors), needle and thread, scissors

4 Stitch a hem along the top of each shape that's big enough to fit your belt through.

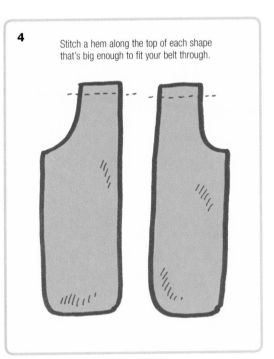

5

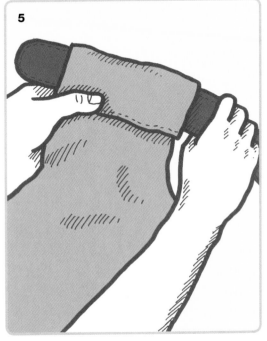

Method:

1 Measure, mark, and cut out two shapes on the felt as shown, 20" long and 6" wide at the widest point.

2 Measure, mark, and cut out four large pockets in felt, each one 4" tall by 5" wide. Sew two pockets, one just above the other, on each of the two larger shapes using tight, neat stitches. Don't forget: you'll need access to the pockets, so don't sew along the top!

3 Measure, mark, and cut out the two smaller pockets (these could prove handy for dildo batteries, condoms, lube, and so on). These should measure 2" square and need to be positioned roughly 2" from the top of the larger pockets on each large shape. Sew into place.

4 Fold down a 2" hem (or big enough for the belt to pass through) on each shape and sew a double row of stitches to secure it fast.

5 Thread the belt through both shapes and you're fit to ride 'em, cowboy.

5.3

Sensual Shoebox

Need something to keep your toys in order?
Something that will slide effortlessly and discreetly
under your bed? Look no further than the
customized shoebox.

Time to Create:
30 minutes

Skill Level:
Beginner

You Will Need:
1 empty shoebox (or larger cardboard box), lightweight cardboard (like from the dry cleaner), velvet, scissors or craft knife, glue, paint or contact paper

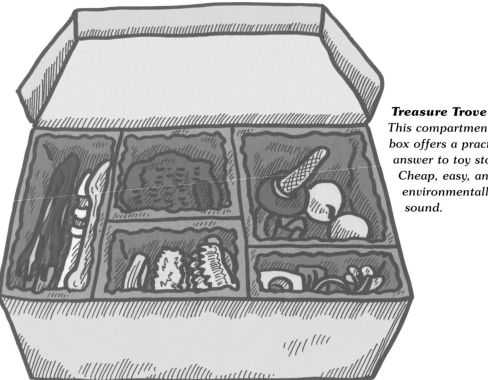

Treasure Trove
This compartmentalized box offers a practical answer to toy storage. Cheap, easy, and environmentally sound.

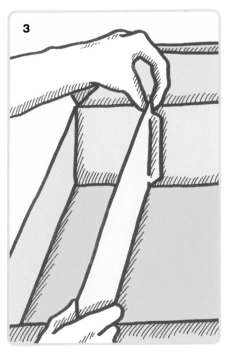

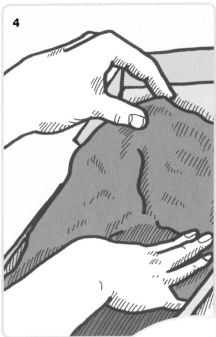

Method:

1 Assess how many toys you need the box to accommodate. Find appropriate box.

2 To make a divider, cut lightweight cardboard to the right length and width, adding an extra half inch to either end where the divider is to meet the box.

3 Lightly score and fold down either end of the divider to form two tabs that will enable easier sticking. Apply glue to the tabs and gently stick in place. Build up a network, if needed, by measuring and sticking dividers.

4 Measure and cut out pieces of velvet to line the insides of each compartment. Glue the sides of the dividers and attach the velvet. Each compartment should feel soft and silky, so it's not important for the velvet to line it exactly.

5 Decorate the exterior with paint, contact paper, or stenciling (see pages 120–1). Your box is now ready.

★ ★ ★

Top Tip

For larger collections (congratulations!), why not stick two shoeboxes together?

★ ★ ★

5.4

Stenciled Swinger

Decorate your boudoir or sex-toy box with some stimulating stencils. A welcome addition to any home (and they certainly beat chintz).

Box of Delights
Designs can be explicit or, like here, more abstract. The results will always be excellent, though.

Time to Create:
2 hours

Skill Level:
Intermediate

You Will Need:
Appropriate imagery (sources could include the Internet, your local library, or your own porn collection), paint and brushes (there are specialist stencil versions, but ordinary acrylic paint and a decent brush should work just as well if you're careful), lightweight cardboard (like from the dry cleaner), a sharp craft knife, spray adhesive, varnish, water

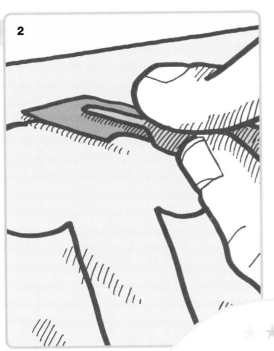

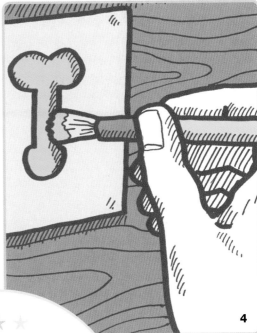

Method:

1 Choose your desired image and enlarge to the size you want (a photocopier's a good bet here). By either using carbon paper or shading heavily in pencil on the back of the copies, trace the imagery onto the cardboard.

2 To make the stencils, cut out the shapes from the cardboard using the craft knife.

3 Position the stencils on top of the object you want to decorate, and fix in place using a little spray adhesive.

★ ★ ★

Top Tip

Preparation! It's undoubtedly a good idea to give yourself plenty of practice before you start. Better to stencil a few pieces of paper than permanently muck up your project.

★ ★ ★

4 Get a small amount of paint onto the brush (too much and the shape will come out globby) and, holding the brush at a 90-degree angle to the surface, gently apply the paint. Once it's dry, you may want to seal it with either varnish or lacquer. Remove the stencil.

5 Et voila—Picasso may not be looking over his shoulder, but that's one hell of a piece of erotica you got there!

5.5

Hanging On In There

This ingenious device is ideal if you want to keep your collection safe and secure in the closet, away from judgment.

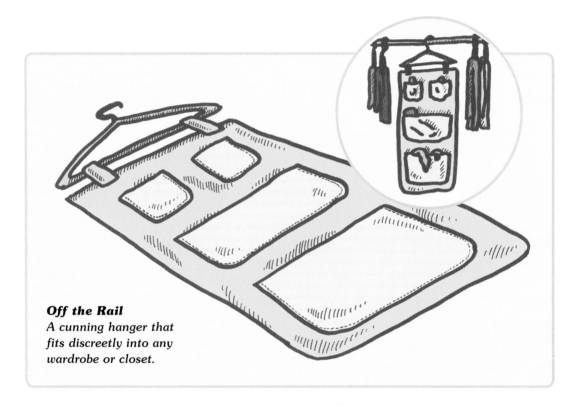

Off the Rail
A cunning hanger that fits discreetly into any wardrobe or closet.

Time to Create:
30 minutes

Skill Level:
Intermediate

You Will Need:
1 coat hanger (wire is OK but wooden ones are stronger), fabric (felt, cotton, rubber, etc.), more material for the pockets, scissors, needle and thread

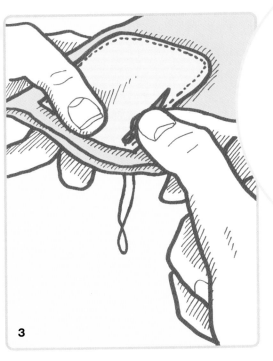

3

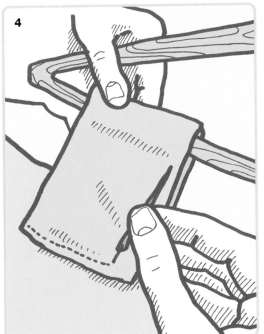

4

Top Tip

Making the pockets out of a translucent or semi-translucent material could aid the process of choosing the right toy for the right joy without the hassle of rifling through each pocket.

★ ★ ★

Method:

1 Assess how big you want the device to be, how many toys it will need to hold, and so on.

2 Measure and cut a piece of fabric to the same width as the coat hanger and the length you want—the example shown is 3' long.

3 Your various-sized pockets should be rectangular, though rounded corners may be more aesthetically pleasing to you. Sew tight, neat stitches close to the pocket edges.

4 Cut out two lengths of fabric that measure 4" long by 1½" wide. Hem and sew about half an inch along all the edges. Place the coat hanger about 2" above the fabric with the pockets face up. Feed each tab up and over the hanger and secure onto the fabric with a double row of stitches.

5 Go hang!

5.6

Repurpose

A simple repurposing of readily available storage solutions may prove invaluably discreet. Just make sure to pass off the right box when your neighbor pops in looking to borrow a screwdriver.

A Hard Day in the Office
They may look innocent enough, but a repurposed tool box or filing cabinet can yield dazzling sex-toy delights. Easy to use and effortlessly clever.

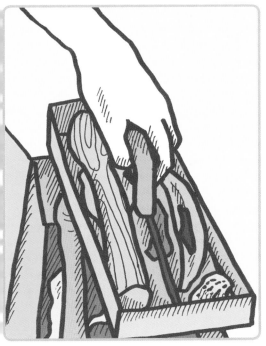

Tool Box: Various models are available from most regular hardware stores. Toughened exteriors will provide valuable protection for your well-made toys, and many have tote trays, which are good for your smaller items like condoms, wet wipes, and so on. Soft-grip handles make them easy and comfortable to carry. Why not customize the box of your choice with some carefully selected erotic stencils, as demonstrated on pages 120–1?

Storage Tower: Commonly used for kitchen items or clothing, storage towers also prove highly effective as sex-toy organizers. If it's on wheels, so much the better—the unit can be moved from one side of the bed to the other for both partners' pleasure. Again, consider stenciling for the personal touch.

Filing Cabinet: OK, so you may not need the big daddies you see in most offices, but mini filing cabinets can hold many of your most treasured toys. There are also handy labeling tabs on each drawer to remind you what lives where.

Edwin G. Seibels, an American insurance clerk, invented the vertical file cabinet in 1898. It is not known whether he made his own sex toys.

Resources

Most of the projects in this book are made from common household items or materials that are easily found at your local craft or hardware store. If you don't want to share your plans to craft a Willy Warmer with the nice saleslady, here are some discreet online resources.

Create for Less

www.createforless.com

Create for Less sells more than 50,000 brand-name craft supplies at wholesale prices and in bulk quantities (if you're feeling generous). Search by brand, holiday, season, theme, occasion, or craft type (warning: "Teste Tickler" yields no results).

Hancock Fabrics

www.hancockfabrics.com

Hancock Fabrics is America's largest fabric store. Need we say more?

Home Depot

www.homedepot.com

An exhaustive resource for tools and hardware, Home Depot's motto is "You can do it. We can help." So let them!

Jo-Ann Fabrics

www.joann.com

Jo-Ann Fabrics sells fabric, trims, adhesives, needlework accessories, and tons of instructional books if you want to learn more about knitting or crochet basics.

M&J Trimming

www.mjtrim.com

Stocked with ribbons, elastic tape, leather, buttons, tassels, and more, M&J sells everything you might need for adding finishing touches to your masterpieces.

Reprodepot Fabrics

www.reprodepotfabrics.com

If you want to get fancy with your fabric, Reprodepot has the best selection of reproduction prints. The fabrics are fun and inspiring (and sold at very good prices).

Index